POPULAR
MUSIC

The Popular Music Series

Popular Music, 1980–1989 is a revised cumulation of and supersedes Volumes 9 through 14 of the *Popular Music* series, all of which are still available:

Volume 9, 1980–84
Volume 10, 1985
Volume 11, 1986

Volume 12, 1987
Volume 13, 1988
Volume 14, 1989

Popular Music, 1920–1979 is also a revised cumulation of and supersedes Volumes 1 through 8 of the *Popular Music* series, of which Volumes 6 through 8 are still available:

Volume 1, 2nd ed., 1950–59
Volume 2, 1940–49
Volume 3, 1960–64
Volume 4, 1930–39

Volume 5, 1920–29
Volume 6, 1965–69
Volume 7, 1970–74
Volume 8, 1975–79

Popular Music, 1900–1919 is a companion volume to the revised cumulation.

This series continues with:

Volume 15, 1990
Volume 16, 1991
Volume 17, 1992
Volume 18, 1993

Volume 19, 1994
Volume 20, 1995
Volume 21, 1996
Volume 22, 1997

Other Books by Bruce Pollock

The Face of Rock and Roll: Images of a Generation

Hipper Than Our Kids?: A Rock and Roll Journal of the Baby Boom Generation

In Their Own Words: Popular Songwriting, 1955–1974

The Rock Song Index: The 7500 Most Important Songs of Rock and Roll

When Rock Was Young: The Heyday of Top 40

When the Music Mattered: Rock in the 1960s

ISSN 0886-442X

VOLUME 22

1997

POPULAR MUSIC

An Annotated Guide to American Popular Songs,
Including Introductory Essay, Lyricists and Composers Index,
Important Performances Index,
Awards Index, and List of Publishers

BRUCE POLLOCK
Editor

GALE

DETROIT • NEW YORK • LONDON

Bruce Pollock, *Editor*

Gale Research Staff

Jolen Marya Gedridge, *Project Editor*
Lawrence W. Baker, *Managing Editor*

Mary Beth Trimper, *Production Director*
Deborah L. Milliken, *Production Assistant*

Cynthia Baldwin, *Production Design Manager*
Barbara J. Yarrow, *Graphic Services Supervisor*

Theresa Rocklin, *Manager, Technical Support Services*
Charles Beaumont, *Programmer/Analyst*

This book is printed on acid-free paper that meets the minimum requirements of American National Standard for Information Sciences—Permanence Paper for Printed Library Materials, ANSI Z39.48-1984.

Library of Congress Catalog Card Number 85-653754
ISBN 0-7876-1392-4
ISSN 0886-442X

Printed in the United States of America

10 9 8 7 6 5 4 3 2 1

Contents

About the Book
and How to Use It

This volume is the twenty-second of a series whose aim is to set down in permanent and practical form a selective, annotated list of the significant popular songs of our times. Other indexes of popular music have either dealt with special areas, such as jazz or theater and film music, or been concerned chiefly with songs that achieved a degree of popularity as measured by the music-business trade indicators, which vary widely in reliability.

Annual Publication Schedule

The first nine volumes in the *Popular Music* series covered sixty-five years of song history in increments of five or ten years. Volume 10 initiated a new annual publication schedule, making background information available as soon as possible after a song achieves prominence. Yearly publication also allows deeper coverage—approximately five hundred songs—with additional details about writers' inspiration, uses of songs, album appearances, and more.

Indexes Provide Additional Access

Three indexes make the valuable information in the song listings even more accessible to users. The Lyricists & Composers Index shows all the songs represented in *Popular Music, 1997,* that are credited to a given individual. The Important Performances Index tells at a glance which albums, musicals, films, television shows, or other media-featured songs are represented in the volume. The "Performer" category—first added to the index as "Vocalist" in the 1986 volume—allows the user to see with which songs an artist has been associated this year. The index is arranged by broad media category, then alphabetically by the show or album title, with the songs listed under each title. Finally, the Awards Index provides a list of the songs nominated for awards by the American Academy of

Motion Picture Arts and Sciences (Academy Award) and the American Academy of Recording Arts and Sciences (Grammy Award). Winning songs are indicated by asterisks.

List of Publishers

The List of Publishers is an alphabetically arranged directory providing addresses—when available—for the publishers of the songs represented in *Popular Music, 1997*. Also noted is the organization handling performance rights for the publisher—in the United States, the American Society of Composers, Authors, and Publishers (ASCAP) or Broadcast Music, Inc. (BMI); in Canada, the Society of Composers, Authors, and Music Publishers of Canada (SOCAN); and in Europe, the Society of European Songwriters and Composers (SESAC).

Tracking Down Information on Songs

Unfortunately, the basic records kept by the active participants in the music business are often casual, inaccurate, and transitory. There is no single source of comprehensive information about popular songs, and those sources that do exist do not publish complete material about even the musical works with which they are directly concerned. Four of the primary proprietors of basic information about our popular music are the major performing rights societies—ASCAP, BMI, SOCAN, and SESAC. Although each of these organizations has considerable information about the songs of its own writer and publisher members and has also issued indexes of its own songs, their files and published indexes are designed primarily for clearance identification by the commercial users of music. Their publications of annual or periodic lists of their "hits" necessarily include only a small fraction of their songs, and the facts given about these are also limited. ASCAP, BMI, SOCAN, and SESAC are, however, invaluable and indispensable sources of data about popular music. It is just that their data and special knowledge are not readily accessible to the researcher.

Another basic source of information about musical compositions and their creators and publishers is the Copyright Office of the Library of Congress. A computerized file lists each published, unpublished, republished, and renewed copyright of songs registered with the Office. It takes between six months and a year from the time of application before songs are officially registered (in some cases, songs have already been released before copyright registration begins). This file is helpful in determining the precise date of the declaration of the original ownership of musical works, but since some authors, composers, and publishers have been known to employ rather makeshift methods of protecting their works legally, there are songs listed in *Popular Music* that may not be found in the Library of Congress files.

Selection Criteria

In preparing the original volumes for this time period, the editor was faced with a number of separate problems. The first and most important of these was that of selection. The stated aim of the project—to offer the user as comprehensive and accurate a listing of significant popular songs as possible—has been the guiding criterion. The purpose has never been to offer a judgment on the quality of any songs or to indulge a prejudice for or against any type of popular music. Rather, it is the purpose of *Popular Music* to document those musical works that (1) achieved a substantial degree of popular acceptance, (2) were exposed to the public in especially notable circumstances, or (3) were accepted and given important performances by influential musical and dramatic artists.

Another problem was whether or not to classify the songs as to type. Most works of music are subject to any number of interpretations and, although it is possible to describe a particular performance, it is more difficult to give a musical composition a label applicable not only to its origin but to its subsequent musical history. In fact, the most significant versions of some songs are often quite at variance with their origins. Citations for such songs in *Popular Music* indicate the important facts about not only their origins but also their subsequent lives, rather than assigning an arbitrary and possibly misleading label.

Research Sources

The principal sources of information for the titles, authors, composers, publishers, and dates of copyright of the songs in this volume were the Copyright Office of the Library of Congress, ASCAP, BMI, SOCAN, SESAC, and individual writers and publishers. Data about best-selling recordings were obtained principally from three of the leading music business trade journals—*Billboard, Radio & Records,* and *Cash Box.* For the historical notes; information about foreign, folk, public domain, and classical origins; and identification of theatrical, film, and television introducers of songs, the editor relied upon collections of album notes, theater programs, sheet music, newspaper and magazine articles, and other material, both his own and that in the Lincoln Center Library for the Performing Arts in New York City.

Contents of a Typical Entry

The primary listing for a song includes

- Title and alternate title(s)
- Country of origin (for non-U.S. songs)
- Author(s) and composer(s)
- Current publisher, copyright date
- Annotation on the song's origins or performance history

Title: The full title and alternate title or titles are given exactly as they appear on the Library of Congress copyright record or, in some cases, the sheet music. Since even a casual perusal of the book reveals considerable variation in spelling and punctuation, it should be noted that these are the colloquialisms of the music trade. The title of a given song as it appears in this series is, in almost all instances, the one under which it is legally registered.

Foreign Origin: If a song is of foreign origin, the primary listing indicates the country of origin after the title. Additional information may be noted, such as the original title, copyright date, writer, publisher in country of origin, or other facts about the adaptation.

Authorship: In all cases, the primary listing reports the author or authors and the composer or composers. The reader may find variations in the spelling of a songwriter's name. This results from the fact that some writers used different forms of their names at different times or in connection with different songs. In addition to this kind of variation in the spelling of writers' names, the reader will also notice that in some cases, where the writer is also the performer, the name as a writer may differ from the form of the name used as a performer.

Publisher: The current publisher is listed. Since *Popular Music* is designed as a practical reference work rather than an academic study, and since copyrights more than occasionally change hands, the current publisher is given instead of the original holder of the copyright. If a publisher has, for some reason, copyrighted a song more than once, the years of the significant copyright subsequent to the year of the original copyright are also listed after the publisher's name.

Annotation: The primary listing mentions significant details about the song's history—the musical, film, or other production in which the song was introduced or featured and, where important, by whom it was introduced, in the case of theater and film songs; any other performers identified with the song; first or best-selling recordings and album inclusions, indicating the performer and the record company; awards; and other relevant data. The name of a performer may be listed differently in connection with different songs, especially over a period of years. The name listed is the form of the name given in connection with a particular performance or record. Dates are provided for important recordings and performances.

Popular Music in 1997

Music historians tend to look at decades as if they were a week on the charts; rabid fans expect each week to bring a year's worth of changes. In truth, while things happen much too fast for all but the trained sprinters to keep up, they actually proceed slowly enough for patterns to emerge that even the armchair observer can make sense of, with the proper perspective. Musical scene sprinters sometimes seem more concerned with keeping up than with appreciating the scenery along the route. They're like the ballplayer who responds to the journalist's earnest summation of his recent unprecedented hitting streak, with a homily on the order of "I don't really look at it that deeply. I'm more interested in tomorrow's game." The journalist, or historian, having written and thought about nearly every game (or popular song) for more than a decade, cares about the nuances of the artform, the ebb and flow of the culture, at least as much as what kinks and wrinkles tomorrow will bring.

In this context, 1997 was one of the more satisfying years in memory for the historian, if not the fan, perfectly epitomizing a succinct yet profound recent truism (perhaps penned by yours truly, but relevant nonetheless). This truism posits that the source of all musical hipness, the roiling wellspring supplying whatever next wave is destined to splash all over the continent, can be invariably found by looking to the distinct creative pools of R&B and England.

Top 40 Revival: Hail to the Queen

As true as it was in the sixties when the Beatles, the Stones and the Yardbirds (and later Led Zeppelin) reinvented the rhythm-and-blues-based rock and roll of the fifties, and in the seventies when punk and funk ruled the artistic curve, or in the eighties when English musicians discovered the synthesizer at the same time that black musicians discovered rap, this concept in the 1990s grew slowly over the last couple of years, until it virtually defined 1997—with the prime beneficiary being a revived Top 40, which has always been more able to accept these forms of music over our own homegrown versions of folk/rock.

Dominant since the late 1980s, the presence of R&B at the top of the charts was no surprise. But the continued outpouring of hip new music from England was unexpected. Evoking a Beatlemania not heard of since the days of the New Kids on the Block, or at least Take That, the Spice Girls led the charge ("Wannabe"), proving to be more than wannabees, with several international hits and a mock rock-documentary following their exploits. If the Spice Girls were regarded as a slight but efficient hit machine, other newly established acts were more reminiscent of the days when the credibility of at least half of classic rock was measured by its English pedigree and accent. Blur ("Song2"), Oasis ("D' You Know What I Mean"), Bush ("Greedy Fly") and especially Radiohead ("Paranoid Android") delivered on their early promise. Chumbawamba ("Tubthumping") and Jamiroquai ("Virtual Insanity") both made belated stateside leaps with smash anthems after prosperous careers abroad. The Chemical Brothers ("Block Rockin' Beats"), White Town ("Your Woman"), and Prodigy ("Breathe," "Firestarter") brought the underground sound of Electronica briefly to the Top 40 surface. The Verve's "Bittersweet Symphony" was a poor man's latter day Rolling Stones epic (borrowing freely from an actual Rolling Stones latter day epic).

The Stones, meanwhile, along with Paul McCartney, Fleetwood Mac (three-fifths of whom are English), and Sir Elton John had major comebacks (with Elton and Bernie Taupin's rewrite of their Marilyn Monroe tribute, "Candle in the Wind," as a eulogy to Diana, Princess of Wales, becoming the best-selling single of all-time). AC/DC ("Dirty Eyes") and Led Zeppelin ("The Girl I Love") cleaned out their vaults to revelatory effect. Ozzy Osbourne was briefly "Back on Earth." In fact, wherever the flag of the British empire was waving, there was a bit of action, from the Ireland of U2 ("Staring at the Sun"), to the Canada of Sarah McLachlan ("Building a Mystery") and Barenaked Ladies ("Brian Wilson"), to the Australia of Savage Garden ("I Want You") to the New Zealand of OMC ("How Bizarre"). Also from England—by way of India—Cornershop ("Brimful of Asha") brought back 1960s era folk/rock with a vengeance (and a sitar).

Equally compelling and artistically diverse was the hit music to be found under the R&B rubric, from the steamy exotic chanteuse Erykah Badu ("On & On") to the streetwise vamping of the mildly erotic Mase ("Feel So Good"). Classic rap made a return this year with notable efforts from Will Smith ("Men in Black") and Heavy D ("Big Daddy"). Missy Elliott made a spirited grab for Latifah's Queen of Hip Hop crown ("Sock It 2 Me"). But the biggest impact was made by Sean "Puffy" Combs, as rapper, writer, producer, and general collaborator and all-purpose eulogizer. His tribute to slain rapper Christopher Wallace, aka The Notorious B.I.G., "I'll Be Missing You," was definitely one of the year's emotional highlights. But with the Fugees' creatively mercurial Wyclef Jean ("Guantanamera"), the resurgent Wu-Tang Clan ("Triumph"), the robust flavorings of Usher ("You Make Me Wanna. . ."), the playfully loquacious Busta Rhymes ("Put Your Hands Where My Eyes Could See"), Next's smooth ("Butta Love") and the steady eminence of Babyface, the genre continues to push the boundaries of what was once perceived as a limited form of expression.

Veteran Rockers and Tributes

On American rock soil, by far the most celebrated acts of the year were ones who've been celebrating with their generation for the past twenty years or more, among them, Bob Dylan ("Cold Irons Bound"), James Taylor ("Line Em Up"), John Fogerty ("Blueboy"), and Fleetwood Mac—two fifths of whom are from Southern California ("Silver Springs"). But if any among the younger generation could prove the lie of Keith Richards' Elvis Costelloian remark that no new act interested him or would even exist in five years, it would have to be Dylan's own offspring, Jakob, and his band the Wallflowers ("One Headlight," "Three Marlenas"). Few expected Everclear ("Everything to Everyone") or the Foo Fighters ("Monkey Wrench") to last that long. A bit more adventurous were Third Eye Blind ("Semi-Charmed Life"), Ben Folds Five ("Brick"), their spiritual cousins The Verve Pipe ("The Freshmen"), the confessional female songwriting extremes of the hypersensitive Fiona Apple ("Criminal") and the Zen Earth mothering Paula Cole ("Where Have All the Cowboys Gone," "I Don't Want to Wait").

Which leads us to the year's big discovery, one that transcends pithy proverbs. Whether or not any of today's latest hit song bands will be around in five years or not, their best songs will be. If 1997 proved anything, it's that great songs will outlast bands anyday—the exception being the bands that can create enough of them so that their extended body of work continues to appeal to several generations. In that context, several songwriters had years that were far more successful any of the year's biggest bands. And overall, the song itself, in tribute albums, cover versions, and movie revivals, made a major comeback as an artform, heartening both those who practice the craft and those who enjoying panning the landscape for hidden gems.

Bob Dylan is the most obvious choice for the year's most recognized songwriting effort. His own new album, *Time out of Mind,* was highly lauded with each track acclaimed, if not revered. From that album, Billy Joel covered "To Make You Feel My Love," while Rod Stewart reached thirty years into the Dylan catalogue to cover "Love Minus Zero/No Limit," on the Princess Diana tribute album. The re-release of the classic Jimi Hendrix album *South Saturn Delta* found a notable version of the rarely covered "Drifter's Escape."

More surprising, if not as critically spectacular, was the return of songs by Burt Bacharach (and partner Hal David)—chiefly by virtue of their appearance in two big ticket movies. On the soundtrack of *My Best Friend's Wedding,* one could hear Mary Chapin Carpenter's version of "I'll Never Fall in Love Again," as well as the incongruous pairing of "Wishin' and Hopin'" with the fiercely feminist icon Ani DiFranco, along with a rousing, nearly anthemic "I Say a Little Prayer." *Austin Powers* did Burt one better, featuring the songwriter himself singing "What the World Needs Now," and even prominently showcasing an album cover from one of his rare ventures into that foreign realm. In the same film, Susannah Hoffs offers a version of "The Look of Love," which was also covered by Sean Lennon and Yuka Honda in the *Great Jewish Music: Burt Bacharach* compilation.

Kurt Weill must be added to the short list of the year's favorite songwriters. Weill's "Alabama Song" received no less than three renditions this year, by Marianne Faithfull, Cameron Silver, and David Johansen, while "September Song" picked up two more, by Lou Reed and Betty Carter. "Ballad of the Soldier's Wife" was recorded by British avant thrush PJ Harvey, as well as Faithfull. Throw in a Nick Cave version of "Mack the Knife" and you have a year that could equal anybody's.

Long known as the "World's Greatest Rock and Roll Band," the Rolling Stones are often overlooked as far as their songwriting prowess. This year the team of Keith Richards and Mick Jagger definitely got their writing due. There were, in fact, *three* Stones tribute albums in 1997, from three different genres, the best of which featured blues musicians like the Holmes Brothers ("Beast of Burden"). The pop tribute found the underappreciated Dramarama resurrecting one of Jagger's finest solo moments ("Memo from Turner" from the film *Performance*). And the country tribute offered Deana Carter's version of "No Expectations." Yet another genre clocked in when Glenn Tipton, late of Judas Priest, offered the heavy metal take on "Paint It Black." Finally, there was Marianne Faithfull's tribute to her former self ("Sister Morphine").

Cover Versions: Stop Me If You've Heard This One. . .

The cover version in general, itself long a forgotten if not reviled pastime, had a fruitful 1997, and not due to any overweening creative apathy on the part of the artists choosing it. Certainly inspired was a triple play like Sublime's take on Bob Marley's "Trenchtown Rock," Warren G.'s version of Marley's "I Shot the Sheriff" and Ziggy Marley's cover of Curtis Mayfield's "People Get Ready." The untimely passing of Laura Nyro coincided not only with a Nyro boxed set, but with a tribute album (*Buy and Sell* by Suzanne Vega). Some of rock's most treasured underground gems were unearthed this year for a younger generation: the Only Ones' "Another Girl, Another Planet," by the Replacements and "That's When I Reach for My Revolver" by Moby. Only slightly less exalted was Iggy Pop's "1969," covered on an Iggy tribute set by Joey Ramone, and the Raspberries' "Overnight Sensation," revived by the Hushdrops.

Rock and roll was by no means the only genre to pay tribute to the fine art of songwriting in this time-honored method. This year the connoisseur could appreciate Susannah McCorkle's diligence in dusting off the 1947 Irving Berlin obscurity "Love and the Weather." Hoagy Carmichael benefitted from the inspired duet by Carly Simon and the ubiquitous John Travolta on "Two Sleepy People." So did Hoagy's co-writer on the song, Frank Loesser, when a Dorothy Lamour reissue brought back his oft-covered "Moon of Manakoora," first heard in the 1937 film *Hurricane.* The songs of Bart Howard ("You Are Not My First Love") received a loving tribute from KT Sullivan. Betty Buckley revived the 1960 Tom Jones-Harvey Schmidt number from *The Fantasticks,* "Much More." From the realms of supper club schtick, who will ever forget the David Frischberg classic, "Peel Me a Grape," done justice this year by Diana Krall, or Tom Lehrer's similarly droll "Rikety Tikety Tin," as revived by Barbara Manning. Active this year was the catalogue of Richard Rodgers and Oscar Hammerstein, with Barbara Cook's version of "The Gentleman Is a Dope," and the TV version of the duo's musical *Cinderella,* which featured Whitney Houston singing "Impossible." Also on that TV special was the Rodgers tune from the 1962 musical *No Strings,* "The Sweetest Sounds," as sung by hip hop thrush Brandy and heartthrob Paola Montalban.

Other R&B acts found plenty to cover as well, with Allure's version of the Lisa Lisa ballad "All Cried Out" and the Az Yet nod to Chicago's "Hard to Say I'm Sorry" leading the way. More inspired, perhaps, were choices made by Prince ("Betcha by Golly, Wow"), Coolio (the 1973 Dramatics' cut, "The Devil Is Dope"), Maxwell (Kate Bush's tearjerker, "This Woman's Work"), Janet Jackson (Rod Stewart's makeout epic,

"Tonight's the Night") or Wyclef Jean (the Pete Seeger freedom fighting anthem, "Guantanamara").

Country folk were just as active in 1997, led by Dwight Yoakam's album of cover tunes, chief among them his tribute to Sonny & Cher's "Baby Don't Go" and Danny O'Keefe's "Good Time Charlie's Got the Blues" and the Jimmie Rodgers tribute album, featuring Willie Nelson's version of "Peach Pickin' Time Down in Georgia," and Steve Earle's take on "In the Jailhouse Now." Then there was Nanci Griffith's cover of Guy Clark's "She Ain't Goin' Nowhere," Willie and Waylon's previously unreleased cover of Steve Earle's "Nowhere Road," Robert Earl Keen's rendition of Dave Alvin's classic "Fourth of July," Alison Kraus' Grammy-winning performance of the Patty Loveless tune, "Looking in the Eyes of Love," the k.d. lang tongue-in-cheek version of the 1948 Peggy Lee gem "Don't Smoke in Bed," and LeAnn Rimes' return to her roots, with the sugary 1977 number, "You Light Up My Life."

On the other hand, none of these could match, for sheer bravado, things like Jane's Addiction doing "Tonight" from *West Side Story,* or Pat Boone trying on the Led Zeppelin perennial, "Stairway to Heaven," or Metallica's "The Unforgiven" as reinterpreted by Apocalyptica with four cellos. As ever (as Knicks' commentator Walt "Clyde" Frazier might say), the cover art astounds even as it confounds.

Nowhere More So Than in the Movies

It is in the movies that you find Woody Allen's virtual tribute album of a movie *Everyone Says I Love You.* Many characters cover old tunes, the standout being Goldie Hawn's stellar version of "I'm Thru with Love." Of course, the crowning, or uncrowning moment, of *The Full Monty* was the Tom Jones over-the-top rendition of Randy Newman's over-the-top classic "You Can Leave Your Hat On," last heard in $9\frac{1}{2}$ *Weeks.* For some, the high point of *Grosse Pointe Blank* was rediscovering the Violent Femme's nugget "Blister in the Sun." Others found that paling beside the news of the re-release of the Mel Brooks movie standard "Springtime for Hitler," and its accompanying soundtrack.

Show-Stopping Ballads and Broadway Bombs

Which is not to say there weren't any great new songs being written in 1997. Even in the predictable realm of filmdom, where predictable big ballads boom from the hearts of overwrought divas (I'm thinking of the Will Jennings/James Horner aria "My Heart Will Go On" from *Titanic,*

R. Kelly's "I Believe I Can Fly" from *Space Jam,* and Diane Warren's "How Do I Live" from *Con Air*), there was the occasional small gem. Here we had the subtle pleasures of Bruce Springsteen's "The Secret Garden," rescued from last year's *Jerry McGuire* soundtrack for a short run on the pop charts this year, or the poignant "C U When You Get There," by soundtrack veteran Coolio, from the otherwise forgettable *Nothing to Lose.* Bush provided the aural excitement for *An American Werewolf in Paris* with "Mouth." And while the competing versions of "How Do I Live" by LeAnn Rimes and Trisha Yearwood made a good story, it was not as good as Elliott W. Smith's five-song breakthrough in *Good Will Hunting,* which included the haunting "Angeles," as well as the Oscar-nominated "Miss Misery."

On Broadway, where great songwriting has been virtually moribund for years, this year we had a plethora of genre-expanding numbers. More of a shipwreck than *Titanic* (the boat, not the movie or the musical), *The Capeman* did produce a score by Paul Simon that was at least on a par with his other failed media experiment (the movie *One-Trick Pony*), including such do-wop flavored Latin rock gems as "Bernadette," "Trailways Bus," and "I Was Born in Puerto Rico." There were show-stopping ballads by Leslie Bricusse and Frank Wildhorn from *Jekyll & Hyde* ("This Is the Moment"), Lynn Ahrens and Stephen Flaherty from *Ragtime* ("Wheels of a Dream"), Bill Russell and Henry Krieger from *Side Show* ("Who Will Love Me as I Am"), and Maury Yeston from *Titanic* ("Godspeed Titanic"). There were smaller, clever items, as well, from off-Broadway oddities like *When Pigs Fly* ("Laughing Matters" by Dick Gallagher), *Secrets Every Smart Traveler Should Know* ("Paradise Found" by Stan Freeman), and *I Love You, You're Perfect, Now Change* ("I Will Be Loved" by Joe DiPietro and Jimmy Roberts). In a class by itself was Steve Schalchlin's stirring autobiographical musical about a musician with AIDS, *The Last Session* ("When You Care").

It Was Quiet in Nashville

Down on Music Row, the neighborhood in Nashville that contains more songwriters per square inch than anywhere else in America, it was, ironically, a rather quiet year, dominated by these closeted professionals, who should perhaps start getting out of the neighborhood more often. Like the regulars at Damon Runyan's Largest Floating Crap Game in New York, the usual Nashville suspects like Don Schlitz ("She Said, He Heard," "Good as I Was to You," "Loved Too Much"), Mark D. Sanders ("This Ain't No Thinkin' Thing," "Come Cryin' to Me," "I'd Rather Ride

Around with You"), Rick Bowles ("Emotional Girl," "A Girl's Gotta Do What a Girl's Gotta Do," "Sittin' on Go"), Trey Bruce ("Amen Kind of Love," "If She Don't Love You," "How Your Love Makes Me Feel"), newcomer Stephony Smith ("Go Away," "How Was I to Know," "It's Your Love"), and the Springers brothers—Roger ("It's a Little Too Late," "Let It Rain," "Thank God for Believers") and Mark Alan ("Thank God for Believers," "When I Close My Eyes," "Where Corn Don't Grow")—took turns rolling the dice for the top numbers on the country charts, each coming away with a similar share of the pie for their occasional interchangeable titles, hooks, concepts, tunes, rhyme schemes, and overall emotional commitment. The exception being Matraca Berg ("Still Holding On," "We Danced Anyway"), who branched out this year with her own album of very personal material ("Back When We Were Beautiful").

Of course, where such an establishment is long entrenched, an underground movement usually percolates, fostering distinct if lonesome (and underpaid) voices. In the nascent Alternative Country scene this year the prolific Steve Earle by far predominated, with his caustic album of folky laments entitled *El Corazon* ("Christmas in Washington," "Taneytown," "Telephone Road"), evoking both Bob Dylan and Woody Guthrie in their primes. The singing, playing and song choices of bluegrass maven Alison Kraus & Union Station ("Find My Way Back to My Heart,") were so pure and stately as to make her an obvious alternative to most commercial country music. Blues singer/songwriter Gillian Welch wrote a standout tune for Suzy Bogguss ("455 Rocket"). Jimmie Dale Gilmour showed his roots rock acumen ("Fourth of July"). From the East (that's Hoboken, not Hong Kong), the Five Chinese Brothers gave us the Dirt Road classic "Let's Kill Saturday Night." And finally, a heartfelt "welcome back" must be given to the country-blues belter Tracy Nelson, whose appearance benefitted a couple of rootsy songs this year ("Is All of This for Me," from the Scotty Moore-DJ Fontana album, and Janis Joplin's "What Good Can Drinkin' Do" from the Joplin tribute album).

Puffy and Babyface Do Their Thing

With no Music Row of its own, now that Motown's Hit Factory has gone the way of New York City's Brill Building, these days the best of R&B songwriting seemed to be coming from the back seat of Sean "Puffy" Combs' limo. A one-man singing-producing-songwriting triple-threat hot commodity, Combs provided Christopher Wallace with some of his best material ("Hypnotize") and had everyone else from Mariah Carey

("Honey") to SWV ("Someone") to Brian McKnight ("You Should Be Mine [Don't Waste Your Time]"), waiting at various stoplights to snatch his latest efforts. And he still managed to save some for himself and that loose consortium known as "The Family" ("It's All About the Benjamins," "Can't Nobody Hold Me Down").

Last year's favorite R&B flavor, Kenny "Babyface" Edmunds, showed no signs of creative meltdown in 1997, with his own smashes like "Everytime I Close My Eyes" and "How Come, How Long", and "I Care 'Bout You" for Milestone, "A Song for Mama" for Boys II Men, "We're Not Making Love No More" for Dru Hill, "Whatever" for En Vogue, and "Best of Love" for Michael Bolton signifying another massive year.

Neither did the favorite R&B songwriting team of the 1990s loosen their grip on the top of the pops. Working with Janet Jackson ("Together Again," "Got Till It's Gone"), Mary J. Blige ("Love Is All We Need," "Everything"), Crystal Waters ("Say. . . If You Feel Alright"), Rod Stewart ("If We Fall in Love Tonight") and Boyz II Men ("4 Seasons of Loneliness"), Terry Lewis and James Harris III managed to put together a lucrative 1997.

With the old school of rap represented by Will Smith, Heavy D, and KRS-One, the new school was taken over this year by the outsized presence of Missy "Misdeanor" Elliot, who scored with "The Rain (Supa Dupa Fly)" and "Sock It 2 Me" for herself, "What About Us" for Total, and "Up Jumps Da Boogie" for her kindred brothers Timbaland and Magoo, and "Not Tonight" for her kindred sisters Lil Kim, Da Brat, Left Eye, and Angie Martinez. For down-to-earth sassiness, Elliott just about has the field to herself, now that R. Kelly has left the playground for the palaces of Hollywood ("I Believe I Can Fly" from Space Jam, "Gotham City" from Batman and Robin).

MmmmBop, Mmmm Cult

Shawn Colvin's double-Grammy win for the brooding "Sunny Came Home" notwithstanding, the death grip Diane Warren has had on pop songwriting honors was hardly dented this year (Monica's "For You I Will," "How Do I Live" with versions by Trisha Yearwood and LeAnn Rimes, "I Turn to You" by All-4-One, "The One I Gave My Heart To" by Brandy, and En Vogue's "Too Gone, Too Long"). But with infectious fluff like "Barbie Girl" by Aqua and "MmmmBop" by Hansen breaking this year, along with the Spice Girl machine ("2 Become 1"), a passing of the torch to much younger hands could foreshadow a youth takeover of the Top 40 not seen since the heyday of Tiffany and Debbie Gibson back in 1987.

With all the talk of a resurgent Top 40, where is America to turn for its own desperately needed underground movement in the midst of this media-frenzied, information-overloaded, 24-hour-news cycle age, where the hip becomes passe in the time it takes to send a sound byte around the globe? Now that every other chart claims a certain numerical credibility, how is a writer to cultivate the kind of inbred obscurity that guarantees living legendhood long after all these one-shot bands have become the stuff of tomorrow's trivia? Used to be a Dan Bern could write "Marilyn" and live in the comfortable squalor of that achievement indefinitely. But now word has it that he's already got a song in the 1998 movie *Zero Effect*. How much longer will cult heroes like Robert Pollard ("Mute Superstar"), Dar Williams ("That's What I Hear in These Sounds"), Lori Carson ("Something's Got Me"), Ira Kaplan and Georgia Hubley ("Autumn Sweater"), Doug Martsch ("Velvet Waltz"), Mark Sandman ("Early to Bed"), Steven Malkmus ("Fin"), Beth Orton ("Live as You Dream") and the feisty Corrin Tucker and Carrie Brownstein ("One More Hour") remain an acquired taste?

For our sake, we hope forever. For theirs, we hope Hollywood calls.

Bruce Pollock
Editor

A

Abuse Me (Australian)
Words and music by Daniel Johns.
Sony ATV Songs, 1997.
Best-selling record by Silverchair from the album *Freak Show* (Epic, 97).

Alabama Song (German)
English words and music by Kurt Weill and Berthold Brecht.
WB Music, 1928.
Revived by Marianne Faithfull on the album *20th Century Blues* (RCA Victor, 97). Also revived by Cameron Silver on the album *Berlin to Babylon* (Entre, 97) and by David Johansen on the album *September Songs- The Music of Kurt Weill* (Sony Classical, 97).

All Cried Out
Words and music by Full Force.
Careers-BMG Music, 1986/Mokajumbi, 1986/Zomba Music, 1986.
Revived by Allure on the album *Allure* (Crave/Track Masters, 97). It was previously a hit for Lisa Lisa & Cult Jam.

All the Good Ones Are Gone
Words and music by Dean Dillon and Bill McDill.
Acuff Rose Music, 1996/Polygram International Music, 1996/Ranger Bob Music, 1996.
Best-selling record by Pam Tillis from the album *Pam Tillis--Greatest Hits* (Arista, 97). Nominated for a Grammy Award, Best Country Song of the Year, 1997.

All I Want
Words and music by Troy Taylor, Charles Farrar, Freddie Perren, Berry Gordy, Deke Richards, and Alfonze Mizell.
Kharatroy Music, 1997/B. Black Music, 1997/Jobete Music Co., 1997/ EMI-April Music, 1997.
Best-selling record by 702 in the film and on the soundtrack album *Good Burger* (Motown, 97).

All Mixed Up
Words and music by Douglas Martinez and Nick Hexum.
Hydroponic Music, Beverly Hills, 1997.
Best-selling record by 311 from the album *311* (Mercury, 96).

All by Myself
Words and music by Eric Carmen and Sergei Rachmaninoff.
Eric Carmen Music, 1976/Songs of Polygram, 1976.
Best-selling record by Celine Dion from the album *Falling into You*
    (550 Music, 96).

All for You
Words and music by Ken Block and Sister Hazel.
Music Corp. of America, 1997/Cherry Music, 1997/Crooked Chimney
    Music, 1997.
Best-selling record by Sister Hazel from the album *Somewhere More
    Familiar* (Universal, 97).

Almost Honest
Words and music by Dave Mustaine and Marty Friedman.
Mustaine Music, 1997/Screen Gems-EMI Music Inc., 1997/Adam
    Martin Music, 1997.
Best-selling record by Megadeth from the album *Cryptic Writings*
    (Capitol, 97).

Alone (English)
Words and music by Barry Gibb, Robin Gibb, and Maurice Gibb.
Careers-BMG Music, 1997/Gibb Brothers Music, 1997.
Best-selling record by the Bee Gees from the album *Still Waters* (A &
    M, 97).

Amen Kind of Love
Words and music by Trey Bruce and Wayne Tester.
MCA Music, 1996.
Best-selling record by Daryle Singletary from the album *All Because of
    You* (Reprise, 96).

Angel in My Eyes
Words and music by Eric Blair Daly and Rich Mullins.
Reynsong Music, 1997/Knob Twister Music, 1997.
Best-selling record by John Michael Montgomery from the album *What
    I Do Best* (Atlantic, 97).

Angeles
Words and music by Elliot Smith.
Careers-BMG Music, 1997/Spent Bullets Music, 1997.
Introduced by Elliot Smith on the album *Either/Or* (Kill Rock Stars,
    97). It is also featured in the film and on the soundtrack *Good Will
    Hunting*.

Another Girl, Another Planet (English)
Words and music by Peter Perrett.
Incomplete Music, 1979.
Revived by The Replacements on the album *Farewell Dinner* (Reprise,
    97). It was a cult/critical favorite introduced by the Only Ones.

Another You
Words and music by Brad Paisley.
EMI-April Music, 1997.
Best-selling record by David Kersh from the album *Goodnight
    Sweetheart* (Curb, 97).

Anybody Seen My Baby (English-Canadian)
Words and music by Mick Jagger, Keith Richards, Ben Mink, and k.d.
    lang.
Promopub B. V., CH-1017 Amsterdam, Netherlands, 1997/Bumstead,
    1997/Polygram International Music, 1997/Zavion, 1997.
Introduced by The Rolling Stones on the album *Bridges to Babylon*
    (Virgin, 97).

At the Beginning
Words and music by Stephen Flaherty and Lynn Ahrens.
TCF Music, 1997.
Best-selling record by Richard Marx and Donna Lewis in the film and
    on the soundtrack album *Anastasia* (Atlantic, 97).

Autumn Sweater
Words and music by Ira Kaplan and Georgia Hubley.
Roshashauna, Hoboken, 1997/Excellent Classical Songs, 1997.
Introduced by Yo La Tengo on the album *I Can Hear the Heart Beating
    as One* (Matador, 97).

Avenues (English)
Words and music by Eddy Grant.
Intersong, USA Inc., 1997/Warner-Chappell Music, 1997.
Revived by Refugee Camp All-Stars featuring Pras (with Ky Mani) on
    the album *Carnival* (Arista, 97). Based on "Electric Avenue" by Eddy
    Grant.

B

Baby Don't Go
Words and music by Sonny Bono.
Ten-East Music, 1965/Mother Bertha Music, Inc., 1965.
Revived by Dwight Yoakam and Sheryl Crow on the album *Under the Covers* (Reprise, 97). Remake of Sonny & Cher's legendary first hit.

Back on Earth (English)
Words and music by Taylor Rhodes and Richard Supa.
MCA Music, 1997.
Best-selling record by Ozzy Osbourne from the album *The Ozzman Cometh* (Epic, 97).

Back When We Were Beautiful
Words and music by Matraca Berg.
Longitude Music, 1997/August Wind Music, 1997/Great Broad Music, 1997.
Introduced by Matraca Berg on the album *Sunday Morning to Saturday Night* (Rising Tide, 97).

Backyard Boogie
Words and music by Dedric Rolison.
WB Music, 1997/Real an Ruff Music, 1997.
Best-selling record by Mack 10 from the album *Based on a True Story* (Priority, 97).

Ballad of the Soldier's Wife (German)
English words and music by Kurt Weill and Berthold Brecht.
WB Music, 1928.
Revived by P. J. Harvey on the album *September Songs--The Music of Kurt Weill* (Sony Classical, 97). Also revised by Marianne Faithfull on the album *20th Century Blues* (RCA, 97).

Barbie Girl (Danish)
English words and music by Soren Rasted, Claus Norreen, Rene Dif, and Lene Grawford Nystrom.

MCA Music, 1997/WB Music, 1997/Warner-Chappell Music, 1997.
Best-selling record by Aqua from the album *Aquarium* (MCA, 97). This
    song sparked a lawsuit from the makers of the Barbie doll, because of
    its "demoralizing" lyrics.

Barely Breathing
Words and music by Duncan Sheik.
Duncan Sheik Music, 1997/Happ Dog Music, 1997/Careers-BMG
    Music, 1997.
Best-selling record by Duncan Sheik from the album *Duncan Sheik*
    (Atlantic, 97). Mid-tempo ballad was on the charts longer than any
    other record in '97.

Battle of Who Could Care Less
Words and music by Ben Folds.
Sony ATV Music, 1997/Fresh Avery Music, 1997.
Introduced by Ben Folds Five on the album *Whatever and Ever, Amen*
    (550 Music/Epic/Caroline, 97). This was from the "Steely Dan of the
    1990s."

Beast of Burden (English)
Words and music by Mick Jagger and Keith Richards.
Colgems-EMI Music, 1978.
Revived by The Holmes Brothers on the album *Paint It Blue--Songs of
    The Rolling Stones* (HOB Music, 97).

Before Today (English)
Words and music by Ben Watt.
Sony ATV Music, 1996.
Revived by Everything but the Girl in the film and on the soundtrack
    album *The Saint* (Virgin, 97).

Bernadette
Words and music by Paul Simon and Derek Walcott.
Paul Simon Music, 1997.
Introduced by Paul Simon on the album *Songs from the Capeman*
    (Warner Brothers, 97). Introduced by Mark Anthony and Sophia
    Salguero in the musical *The Capeman*.

Best of Love
Words and music by Michael Bolton and Babyface (pseudonym for
    Kenny Edmunds).
Mr. Bolton's Music, 1997/Warner-Chappell Music, 1997/Warner-
    Tamerlane Music, 1997/Sony ATV Songs, 1997/Ecaf Music, 1997.
Best-selling record by Michael Bolton from the album *All That Matters*
    (Columbia, 97).

Betcha by Golly Wow
Words and music by Thom Bell and Linda Creed.

Assorted Music, 1970/Bellboy Music, 1970.
Revived by Prince (Artist Formerly Known As) on the album
Emancipation (NPG, 96). Philly soul standard.

Better Man, Better Off
Words and music by Bill Jones and Stanley Paul David.
Ensign Music, 1997/Shoot Straight Music, 1997.
Best-selling record by Tracy Lawrence from the album *The Coast Is
Clear* (Atlantic, 97).

Between the Covers
Words and music by Cris Williamson.
Bird Ankles Music, 1997.
Introduced by Cris Williamson and Tret Fure on the album *Between the
Covers* (Wolf Moon/Goldenrod, 97).

Between the Devil and Me
Words and music by Harley Allen and Carson Chamberlain.
Coburn Music, 1996/Ten Ten Tunes, 1996/Polygram Music Publishing
Inc., 1996/Colt-N-Twins Music, 1996.
Best-selling record by Alan Jackson from the album *Everything I Love*
(Arista Nashville, 97).

Big Bad Mamma
Words and music by Samuel Barnes, Jean Claude Olivier, Sean Carter,
and Leon Haywood.
American Romance Music, Nashville, 1997/Slam U Well Music, 1997/
Lil Lu Lu Music, 1997/Jim-Edd Music, 1997/712 Stone Avenue
Music, 1997/EMI-Blackwood Music Inc., 1997/Jumping Bean Music,
1997/Jelly's Jams L.L.C. Music, 1997.
Best-selling record by Foxy Brown featuring Dru Hill in the film and on
the soundtrack album *How to Be a Player* (Mercury, 97).

Big Daddy
Words and music by Tony Dofat and Heavy D (pseudonym for Dwight
Myers).
Dofat Music, 1997/Soul on Soul Music, 1997/EMI-April Music, 1997/
Reifman Music, 1997.
Best-selling record by Heavy D from the album *Waterbed Hev*
(Universal, 97).

Bitch
Words and music by Meredith Brooks and Shelby Peiken.
Kissing Booth Music, 1997/Warner-Tamerlane Music, 1997/Hidden Pun
Music, 1997/Sushi Too Music, 1997.
Best-selling record by Meredith Brooks from the album *Blurring the
Edges* (Capitol, 97). Nominated for a Grammy Award, Best Rock
Song of the Year, 1997.

Bitter
Words and music by Jill Sobule and Richard Barone.
I'll Show You Music, 1997/Warner-Chappell Music, 1997/Richard
   Barone Music, 1997.
Introduced by Jill Sobule on the album *Happy Town* (Lava/Atlantic, 97).

Bittersweet Symphony (English)
Words and music by Mick Jagger, Keith Richards, and Richard
   Ashcroft.
ABKCO Music Inc., 1997.
Best-selling record by The Verve from the album *Urban Hymns* (Virgin,
   97). This was the college rock song of the year.

Black Hole Sun
Words and music by Chris Cornell.
You Make Me Sick, I Make Music, 1994.
Revived by Steve Lawrence and Eydie Gorme on the album
   Loungeapalooza (Hollywood, 97).

Black Patch
Words and music by Laura Nyro.
EMI-Blackwood Music Inc., 1970.
Revised by The 5th Dimension on the album *Up Up and Away--The
   Definitive Collection* (Arista, 97).

Blister in the Sun
Words and music by Gordon Gano.
Gorno Music, 1982.
Revived by The Violent Femmes in the film and on the soundtrack
   album *Grosse Pointe Blank* (London, 97).

Block Rockin' Beats (English)
Words and music by Tom Rowlands, Ed Simons, and Jesse Weaver.
Sony ATV Songs, 1997.
Best-selling record by The Chemical Brothers from the album *Dig Your
   Own Hole* (Astralwerks/Caroline, 97). This song introduced the year's
   electronica craze.

Blueboy
Words and music by John C. Fogerty.
Cody River Music, Sherman Oaks, 1997.
Introduced by John Fogerty on the album *Blue Moon Swamp* (Warner
   Brothers, 97).

Brazil
Words and music by Patty Larkin.
BMG Songs Inc., 1997/No Chapeau, 1997/Lamartine, 1997.
Introduced by Patty Larkin on the album *Perishable Fruit* (High Street,
   97).

Break My Stride
Words and music by Matthew Wilder and Greg Prestopino.
Streetwise Music, 1983/Buchu Music, 1983/No Ears Music, 1983.
Revived by Unique II (Columbia, 97). It was also revived by Max-a-Million (Baby O, 97).

Breaking All the Rules (German)
English words and music by Frank Beermann, Christian Beermann, Jeff Coplan, and Matthew Dexter.
Shark Music, 1997/Warner-Tamerlane Music, 1997/Humassive Music, 1997.
Best-selling record by She Moves from the album *Breaking All the Rules* (Geffen, 97).

Breathe (English)
Words and music by Liam Howlett, Keith Flint, and Maxim Palmer.
Virgin Music, 1997.
Best-selling record by Prodigy from the album *Fat of the Land* (Mute/Maverick, 97).

Brian Wilson (Canadian)
Words and music by Stephen Page.
Treat Baker Music, 1994/WB Music, 1994.
Revived by Barenaked Ladies on the album *Rock Spectacle* (Reprise, 97). This was a tongue-in-cheek tribute to the reclusive Beach Boy.

Brick
Words and music by Ben Folds and Darren Jessee.
Sony ATV Songs, 1997/Fresh Avery Music, 1997.
Best-selling record by Ben Folds Five from the album *Whatever and Ever, Amen* (550 Music/Epic/Caroline, 97).

Brimful of Asha (English)
Words and music by Tjinder Singh.
American Momentum, Burbank, 1997/Wiija (England), 1997.
Best-selling record by Cornershop from the album *When I Was Born for the 7th Time* (Luaka Bop/Warner Brothers, 97). From India by way of England, raga rock is revisited.

A Broken Wing
Words and music by James House, Sam Hogin, and Phil Barnhart.
Sony ATV Tree Publishing, 1997/Sam's Jammin Music, 1997/Suffer in Silence Music, 1997.
Best-selling record by Martina McBride from the album *Evolution* (RCA, 97).

Building a Mystery (Canadian)
Words and music by Sarah McLachlan and Pierre Marchand.
Sony ATV Songs, 1997/Studio Nomado Music, 1997.

Best-selling record by Sarah McLachlan from the album *Surfacing* (Arista, 97). It was a breakthrough year for the creator of the Lilith leader tour.

Busy Child
Words and music by Ken Jordan and Scott Kirkland.
Virgin Music, 1997/Drug Money Music, 1997.
Best-selling record by the Crystal Method from the album *Vegas* (Outpost/Geffen, 97).

Butta Love
Words and music by Lance Alexander, Tony Tolbert, Robert Huggar, Arkieda Clowers, and Darren Lighty.
Honey Jars & Diapers Music, 1997/Uh-Oh Music, 1997/Yah Yah Music, 1997/Do What I Gotta Music, 1997.
Best-selling record by Next from the album *Rated Next* (Arista, 97).

Butterfly Kisses
Words and music by Bob Carlisle and Randy Thomas.
Polygram International Music, 1997/Diadem Music, 1997.
Best-selling record by the Raybon Brothers from the album *The Raybon Brothers* (MCA, 97). Also best-selling record by Bob Carlisle from the album *Butterfly Kisses (Shades of Grace)* (Jive, 97) and recorded by Jeff Carson on the album *Butterfly Kisses* (Warner Brothers, 97). It was considered this year's most sentimental song. Won a Grammy Award for Best Country Song of the Year 1997.

Buy and Sell
Words and music by Laura Nyro.
EMI-Blackwood Music Inc., 1966.
Revived by Suzanne Vega on the album *Time and Love--The Music of Laura Nyro* (Astor Place, 97). It was from the tribute album that anticipated Nyro's early death from cancer.

C

C U When U Get There
Words and music by Artis Ivey, Jr., Dominick Aldridge, Henry
  Straughter, and Maleek Straughter.
Flying Rabbi Music, Seattle, 1997/Du It All Music, 1997/Lek Ratt
  Music, 1997/Pookie Straughter Music, 1997.
Best-selling record by Coolio and the 40 Thevz in the film and on the
  soundtrack album *Nothing to Lose* (Tommy Boy, 97). It was created
  in the poignant mode of "Gangsta's Paradise."

Call Me (German)
English words and music by Nosie Katzmann, Amir Saraf, Milsar,
  Wagennecht, and Robert Haynes.
Warner-Chappell Music, 1997/Edition, 1997/Get Into Magic, 1997/
  Edition Beam Music, 1997/Private Area, 1997.
Best-selling record by Le Click from the album *Le Click* (RCA, 97).

Candle in the Wind 1997 (English)
Words and music by Elton John and Bernie Taupin.
Polygram Music Publishing Inc., 1973.
Revived by Elton John (A & M, 97). One of the best (and fastest)-
  selling single in history, which was rewritten to eulogize Diana,
  Princess of Wales. All of the proceeds went to the charitable
  organizations she supported.

Can't Nobody Hold Me Down
Words and music by Sean "Puffy" Combs, Steve Jordan, Carlos Brody,
  Nashiel Myrick, Mason Betha, Greg Prestopino, Matthew Wilder, and
  Sylvia Robinson.
Justin Combs Music, 1997/EMI-April Music, 1997/Amani Music, 1997/
  July Six Music, 1997/NASHMACK Music, 1997/Mason Betha Music,
  1997/Buchu Music, 1997/No Ears Music, 1997.
Best-selling record by Puff Daddy & the Family (featuring Mase) from
  the album *No Way Out* (Arista, 97). This characterized Puff's
  breakthrough year.

Carolina Blues
Words and music by John Popper and Chan Kinchla.
Irving Music Inc., 1997.
Introduced by Blues Traveler on the album *Straight on Till Morning* (A & M, 97).

Carrying Your Love with Me
Words and music by Jeff Stevens and Steve Bogard.
Warner-Tamerlane Music, 1997/Rancho Belita Music, 1997/Jeff Stevens Music.
Best-selling record by George Strait from the album *Carrying Your Love with Me* (MCA Nashville, 97).

A Change
Words and music by Sheryl Crow, Jeff Trott, and Brian McLeod.
Old Crow, Los Angeles, 1996/Warner-Tamerlane Music, 1996/Weenie Stand Music, 1996/Trottsky Music, 1996.
Best-selling record by Sheryl Crow from the album *Sheryl Crow* (A & M, 96).

Christmas in Washington
Words and music by Steve Earle.
South Nashville Music, 1997/WB Music, 1997.
Introduced by Steve Earle on the album *El Corazon* (Warner Brothers, 97).

Christmas Wrapping
Words and music by Chris Butler.
Merovingian Music, 1981.
Revived by The Waitresses on the album *Live '82* (King Biscuit, 97). Lead singer Patty Donohue died in '96.

Circle of Life (English)
Words and music by Elton John and Tim Rice.
Wonderland Music, 1994.
Revived by Tsidii Le Loka and Ensemble in the musical and on the cast album *The Lion King* (Walt Disney, 97). The animated movie made a smash transition to Broadway.

Cities
Words and music by David Byrne.
Bleu Disque Music, 1979.
Revived by Phish on the album *Slip Stitch and Pass* (A & M, 97). It was a Talking Heads favorite.

Claudette
Words and music by Roy Orbison.
Roy Orbison Music, 1957/Polygram Music Publishing Inc., 1957/ Barbara Orbison Music, 1997.

Revived by Dwight Yoakam on the album *Under the Covers* (Reprise, 97). This song was written by Roy Orbison and previously performed by the Everly Brothers.

Coco Jamboo (German)
English words and music by Rainer Gaffrey, Kat Matthiesen, and Delroy Rennalls.
Hanseatic Musikverlag GmbH, 2000 Hamburg13, Germany, 1997/ Warner-Tamerlane Music, 1997.
Best-selling record by Mr. President from the album *Mr. President* (Warner Brothers, 97).

Coconut
Words and music by Harry Nilsson.
EMI-Blackwood Music Inc., 1972.
The Harry Nilsson classic was revived in the film and on the soundtrack album *The Ice Storm* (Real Sounds/Velvel, 97).

Cold Irons Bound
Words and music by Bob Dylan.
Special Rider Music, 1997.
Introduced by Bob Dylan his on bleak but triumphant comeback album *Time out of Mind* (Columbia, 97).

Come Cryin' to Me
Words and music by John Rich, Wally Wilson, and Mark D. Sanders.
Sony ATV Tree Publishing, 1997/Feed Them Kids Music, 1997/ Starstruck Angel Music, 1997/Mark D. Music.
Best-selling record by Lonestar from the album *Crazy Nights* (BNA, 97).

Come on Eileen (English)
Words and music by Kevin Rowland, Jim Paterson, and Kevin Adams.
Colgems-EMI Music, 1982.
Revived by Save Ferris on the album *It Means Everything* (Epic, 97).

Confrontation (American-English)
Words and music by Leslie Bricusse and Frank Wildhorn.
Cherry River Music Co., 1995/Stage-Screen Music, Inc., 1995.
Introduced by Robert Cuccioli in the musical and on the cast album *Jekyll & Hyde* (Atlantic Theater, 97). A duet for one, with two masks.

Count Me In
Words and music by Deana Carter and Chuck Jones.
Hamstein Cumberland, Nashville, 1996/Fugue Music, Austin, 1996/EMI-Princeton Street Music, 1996.
Best-selling record by Deana Carter from the album *Did I Shave My Legs for This* (Capitol Nashville, 96).

Counting Blue Cars
Words and music by Scott Alexander, Rodney Browning, Gregory
  Kolanek, John Richards, and George Pendergast.
Mono Rat Music, 1995/Bigger Than Peanut Butter Music, 1995/EMI-
  April Music, 1995.
Best-selling record by Dishwalla from the album *Pet Your Friends* (A &
  M, 95).

Crash into Me
Words and music by Dave Matthews.
David Matthews Music, New York, 1996.
Best-selling record by The Dave Matthews Band from the album *Crash*
  (RCA, 96). Nominated for a Grammy Award, Best Rock Song of the
  Year, 1997.

Criminal
Words and music by Fiona Apple.
FHW Music, Beverly Hills, 1996.
Best-selling record by Fiona Apple from the album *Tidal* (Work Group,
  96). Nominated for a Grammy Award, Best Rock Song of the Year,
  1997.

Cupid
Words and music by Arnold Hennings, Courtney Sills, Daron Jones,
  Michael Keith, Marvin Scandrick, and Quinnes Parker.
Am Music, 1996/EMI-April Music, 1996/Beane Tribe Music, 1996/C.
  Sills Music, 1996/Kevin Wales, 1996/Justin Combs Music, 1996.
Best-selling record by 112 from the album *112* (Arista, 96).

D

D' You Know What I Mean (English)
Words and music by Noel Gallagher.
Creation Music, 1997/Sony ATV Songs, 1997.
Best-selling record by Oasis from the album *Be Here Now* (Epic, 97).

Da Da Da I Don't Love You You Don't Love Me (German)
English words and music by Gert Krawinkel and Stefan Remmler.
Colgems-EMI Music, 1983.
Revived by Trio in a Volkswagen commercial, and then on the album
  Trio (Mercury Chronicles, 97).

Da' Dip
Words and music by Eric Timmons.
Eric Timmons Music, 1997/EMI-Blackwood Music Inc., 1997.
Best-selling record by Freak Nasty from the album *Controversee That's
  Life...And That's the Way It Is* (Triad, 97).

Dance Hall Days (English)
Words and music by Chris Hughes, Ross Cullum, and Darren Costin.
Chong, England, 1985/Warner-Tamerlane Music, 1985.
Revived by Wang Chung on the album *Everybody Wang Chung Tonight*
  (Geffen, 97).

Dancin', Shaggin' on the Boulevard
Words and music by Randy Owen, Teddy Gentry, and Greg Fowler.
Maypop Music, 1997.
Best-selling record by Alabama from the album *Dancin' on the
  Boulevard* (RCA, 97).

Daydream
Words and music by John Sebastian.
Alley Music, 1966/Trio Music Co., Inc., 1997.
Revived by Art Garfunkel on the album *Songs from a Parent to a Child*
  (Sony Wonder/Columbia, 97).

Desperately Wanting
Words and music by Kevin Griffin.
Tentative Music, New Orleans, 1997/Warner-Tamerlane Music, 1997.
Best-selling record by Better Than Ezra from the album *Friction, Baby*
   (Elektra, 97).

Deuce and a Quarter
Words and music by Kevin Gordon and Gwil Owens.
Turgid Tunes, 1997/Bug Music, 1997/Little Rain Music, 1997.
Introduced by Keith Richards on the album *Scotty Moore and DJ
   Fontana--All the King's Men* (Sweetfish, 97). Celebrating two
   essential components of Elvis Presley's original band.

The Devil Is Dope
Words and music by Anthony Hester.
Longitude Music, 1973.
Revived by Coolio with The Dramatics on the album *My Soul* (Tommy
   Boy, 97). This is a tribute to a song that was an early influence.

Did I Shave My Legs for This
Words and music by Deana Carter and Rhonda Hart.
Polygram International Music, 1996/Millermo Music, 1996.
Best-selling record by Deana Carter from the album *Did I Shave My
   Legs for This* (Capital Nashville, 97). This was Nashville's feminist
   statement of the year. Nominated for a Grammy Award, Best Country
   Song of the Year, 1997.

The Difference
Words and music by Jakob Dylan.
Brother Jumbo Music, 1996.
Best-selling record by the Wallflowers from the album *Bringing Down
   the Horse* (Interscope, 97). Nominated for a Grammy Award, Best
   Rock Song of the Year, 1997.

Dirty Eyes (English)
Words and music by Angus Young, Malcolm Young, and Bon Scott.
J. Albert & Sons Music, 1977.
Introduced by AC/DC on the album *Bonfire* (East/West, 97). Early use
   of the classic "Whole Lotta Rosie" riff, finally released this year on
   the Bon Scott tribute record.

Discotheque (Irish)
Words and music by U2, Bono (pseudonym for Paul Hewson), and The
   Edge (pseudonym for Dave Evans).
Polygram International Music, 1997.
Best-selling record by U2 from the album *Pop* (Island, 97).

Do You Know (What It Takes) (Swedish-German)
English words and music by Robyn Carlsson, Denniz Pop, Max Martin,

and Herbert Crichlow.
Heavy Rotation Music, 1997/BMG Music, 1997/Cheiron Music, 1997/
   Megasongs, 1997.
Best-selling record by Robyn from the album *Robyn Is Here* (RCA, 97).

Do You Like This
Words and music by Jerome Woods and Gerald Baillergeau.
Mike's Rap Music, Valencia, 1997.
Best-selling record by Rome from the album *Rome* (RCA, 97).

Don't Cry for Me Argentina (English)
Words and music by Tim Rice and Andrew Lloyd Webber.
MCA Music, 1975.
Revived by Madonna in the film and on the soundtrack album *Evita*
   (Warner Brothers, 97).

Don't Forget Me
Words and music by Harry Nilsson.
EMI-Blackwood Music Inc., 1974.
Revived by Marianne Faithfull on the album *20th Century Blues* (RCA
   Victor, 97).

Don't Give That Girl a Gun
Words and music by Amy Ray.
Virgin Music, 1997/Godhap Music, 1997.
Introduced by The Indigo Girls on the album *Shaming of the Sun* (Epic,
   97).

Don't Go Away (English)
Words and music by Noel Gallagher.
Creation Music, 1997/Sony ATV Songs, 1997.
Best-selling record by Oasis from the album *Be Here Now* (Epic, 97).

Don't Smoke in Bed
Words and music by Willard Robison.
MCA Music, 1948.
Revived by k.d. lang on the album *Drag* (Warner Brothers, 97). This
   was popularized by Peggy Lee.

Don't Speak
Words and music by Gwen Stefani and Eric Stefani.
WB Music, 1996.
Best-selling record and grammy-nominated song by No Doubt from the
   album *Tragic Kingdom* (Warner Brothers, 96). Revived by Clueless
   (ZYX, 97) in the dance version. Nominated for a Grammy Award,
   Best Song of the Year, 1997.

Don't Take Her She's All I Got
Words and music by Jerry Williams and Gary U.S. Bonds.

Jerry Williams Music, 1971/Bug Music, 1971/Embassy Music Corp., 1971/Excellorec Music Co., Inc., 1971.
Revived by Tracy Byrd on the album *Big Love* (MCA, 97). This was originally a hit for Johnny Paycheck.

Don't Wanna Be a Player
Words and music by Joe Thomas, Jolyon Skinner, Rodney Jerkins, Japhe Tejeda, and Michele Williams.
Zomba Music, 1997/Kiely Music, 1997/Conversation Tee Music, 1997/ EMI-Blackwood Music Inc., 1997/Rodney Jerkins Music, 1997/Foray, 1997/1972 Music, 1997/Henchmen Music, 1997.
Best-selling record by Joe in the film and on the soundtrack album *Booty Call* (Jive, 97).

Dream
Words and music by Karl Stephenson, Jaspr Baj, and Kevin Krakower.
BMG Music, 1997.
Introduced by Forest for the Trees on the album *Forest for the Trees* (DreamWorks, 97). Stevenson wrote music and lyrics with Beck.

Drifter's Escape
Words and music by Bob Dylan.
Dwarf Music Co., Inc., 1968.
Reissued by Jimi Hendrix on the album *South Saturn Delta* (MCA/ Experience/Hendrix, 97).

Drink, Swear, Steal & Lie
Words and music by Michael Peterson and Paula Carpenter.
Warner-Tamerlane Music, 1997/BMG Music, 1997/Above the Rim Music, 1997.
Best-selling record by Michael Peterson from the album *Michael Peterson* (Reprise, 97).

E

Early to Bed
Words and music by Mark Sandman.
Pubco Music, Ardmore, 1997/Head with Wings Music, 1997.
Introduced by Morphine on the album *Like Swimming* (Dreamwork/
    Rykodisc, 97).

Easy Money
Words and music by Cy Coleman and Ira Gasman.
Notable Music Co., Inc., 1995/Warner-Chappell Music, 1995.
Introduced by Sam Harris in the musical and on the cast album *The Life*
    (Sony Classical, 97).

Emotional Girl
Words and music by Rick Bowles, Terri Clark, and Chris Waters.
Starstruck Angel Music, 1996/Dead Solid Perfect Music, 1996/Chris
    Waters Music, 1996/Sony ATV Tree Publishing, 1996.
Best-selling record by Terri Clark from the album *Just the Same*
    (Mercury Nashville, 96).

The End Is the Beginning Is the End
Words and music by Billy Corgan.
Chrysalis Music Group, 1997/Cinderful Music, 1997.
Best-selling record by Smashing Pumpkins in the film and on the
    soundtrack album *Batman and Robin* (Warner Brothers, 97).

The End of Something
Words and music by Henry Rollins.
Rok Legend Musik, Los Angeles, 1997/Nineteenoro Music, New York,
    1997.
Introduced by Henry Rollins on the album *Come in and Burn*
    (Dreamworks, 97).

Everlong
Words and music by Dave Grohl.
MJ12 Music, 1997.

Best-selling record by the Foo Fighters from the album *The Colour and the Shape* (Rosswell/Capitol, 97).

Everyday Is a Winding Road
Words and music by Sheryl Crow, Jeff Trott, and Brian MacLeod.
Old Crow, Los Angeles, 1996/Warner-Tamerlane Music, 1996/Trottsky Music, 1996/Wixen Music, 1996/Weenie Stand Music, 1996.
Best-selling record by Sheryl Crow from the album *Sheryl Crow* (A & M, 96). Nominated for a Grammy Award, Best Record of the Year, 1997.

Everything
Words and music by James Harris, III, Terry Lewis, Rokosuke El, Hachidai Nakamura, Thom Bell, Linda Creed, James Brown, and Fred Wesley.
EMI-April Music, 1997/Flyte Tyme Tunes, 1997/Warner-Tamerlane Music, 1997/Dynatone Music, 1997/Beechwood Music, 1997.
Best-selling record by Mary J. Blige from the album *Share My World* (MCA, 97).

Everything to Everyone
Words and music by Arthur Alexakis and Everclear.
Evergleam Music, 1997/Common Green Music, 1997/Montalupis Music, 1997.
Best-selling record by Everclear from the album *So Much for the Afterglow* (Capitol, 97).

Everything I Love
Words and music by Harley Allen and Carson Chamberlain.
Coburn Music, 1996/Ten Ten Tunes, 1996/Just Cuts Music, 1996/Songs of Polygram, 1996.
Best-selling record by Alan Jackson from the album *Everything I Love* (Arista Nashville, 96).

Everytime I Close My Eyes
Words and music by Babyface (pseudonym for Kenny Edmunds).
Sony ATV Songs, 1996/Ecaf Music, 1996.
Best-selling record by Babyface from the album *The Day* (Epic, 96).

Everywhere
Words and music by Craig Wiseman and Mike Reid.
Almo Music Corp., 1997/Daddy Rabbitt Music, 1997/Brio Blues Music, 1997.
Best-selling record by Tim McGraw from the album *Everywhere* (Curb, 97).

F

Falling
Words and music by Lenny LeBlanc and Edward Struzick.
Buddy Killen Music, Nashville, 1977/Asleep in the Boat Music, 1977.
Revived by the Raybon Brothers with Olivia Newton-John on the album
The Raybon Brothers (MCA, 97).

Falling in Love (Is Hard on the Knees)
Words and music by Steven Tyler, Joe Perry, and Glen Ballard.
Swag Song Music, 1997/Aerostation Corp., 1997/MCA Music, 1997.
Best-selling record by Aerosmith from the album *Nine Lives* (Columbia,
97).

Father of Our Nation
Words and music by Cedric Samson.
Introduced by Jennifer Jones and Hugh Masekela in the film *Mandela*.

Feel So Good
Words and music by Kool & the Gang, Larry Dermer, Joey Galdo, and
Rafael Vigil.
Second Decade Music, 1997/Warner-Tamerlane Music, 1997/Foreign
Imported, 1997.
Best-selling record by Mase in the film and on the soundtrack album
Money Talks (Arista, 97). This soundtrack took music samples from
Kool & the Gang's "Hollywood Swinging." It was also featured in
Harlem World (Arista, 97).

Fin
Words and music by Stephen Malkmus.
Virgin Music, 1997/Treble Kicker Music, 1997.
Introduced by Pavement on the album *Brighten the Corners* (Matador,
97).

Find My Way Back to My Heart
Words and music by Mark Stamos.
Devachan Music, Watertown, 1997/Happy Valley Music, 1997.

Introduced by Alison Kraus & Union Station on the album *So Long So Wrong* (Rounder, 97).

Fire Down Below
Words and music by Mark Collie and Steven Seagal.
Pioneer Publishing, Los Angeles, 1997/Snow Lion Music, Los Angeles, 1997/Leiper's Fork Music, 1997.
Introduced by Mark Collie, Aaron Tippin & Jeff Wood in the film and on the soundtrack album *Fire Down Below* (Warner Brothers, 97).

Firestarter (English)
Words and music by Liam Howlett, Keith Flint, Trevor Horn, Anne Dudley, Jonathan Jeczalik, Paul Morley, Greg Langan, and Kim Deal.
Virgin Music, 1997/Unforgettable Songs, 1997/Perfect Songs Music, 1997/Zomba Music, 1997/MCA Music, 1997.
Best-selling record by Prodigy from the album *Fat of the Land* (Warner Brothers, 97).

Fishing
Words and music by Richard Shindell.
Richard Shindell Music, Chesterfield, 1994.
Revived by Joan Baez on the album *Gone from Danger* (Guardian/Angel, 97).

5 Miles to Empty
Words and music by Nichole Gilbert, Big Yam, and Victor Merritt.
Mike's Rap Music, Valencia, 1997/Diamond Cuts Music, 1997/Brown Girl Music, 1997.
Best-selling record by Brownstone from the album *Still Climbing* (Work, 97).

Flowers
Words and music by Billy Yates and Monty Criswell.
Hamstein Cumberland, Nashville, 1997/Music Corp. of America, 1997/So Bizzy Music, 1997/Hillbillion Music, 1997.
Best-selling record by Billy Yates from the album *Billy Yates* (Almo Sounds, 97). This was Nashville's weeper of the year.

Fly
Words and music by William Maragh and Sugar Ray.
Warner-Chappell Music, 1997.
Best-selling record by Sugar Ray from the album *Floored* (Atlantic, 97).

The Fool
Words and music by Marla Cannon, Charlie Stefl, and Gene Ellsworth.
Major Bob Music, 1997/St. Myrna Music, 1997/Castle Bound Music, 1997/Mountain Thyme Music, 1997.
Best-selling record by Lee Ann Womack from the album *Lee Ann Womack* (Decca, 97).

Foolish Games
Words and music by Jewel Kilcher.
WB Music, 1996.
Best-selling record by Jewel in the film and on the soundtrack album
Batman and Robin (Warner Sunset/Atlantic, 96).

For the First Time
Words and music by Jud Friedman, James Newton Howard, and Allan
Rich.
TLC Music, Studio City, 1996/E. B. Marks Music Corp., 1996/Big Fig
Music, 1996/Nelana Music, 1996/Peer Music, 1996/Schmoogietunes,
1996.
Best-selling record by Kenny Loggins from the album *Yesterday, Today,
Tomorrow--Greatest Hits of Kenny Loggins* (Columbia, 97). The 1996
Oscar nominee from the movie *One Fine Day* scored on the ballad
chart.

For Once in Our Lives (English)
Words and music by Chris Difford and Paul Carrack.
Plangent Visions Music, Inc., London, England, 1997/Virgin Music,
1997.
Best-selling record by Paul Carrack from the album *Blue Views* (Ark 21,
97).

For You
Words and music by Kenny Lerum.
Colour'd Music, 1997/PSO Music, 1997.
Best-selling record by Kenny Lattimore from the album *Kenny
Lattimore* (Columbia, 97).

For You I Will
Words and music by Diane Warren.
Realsongs, 1997.
Best-selling record by Monica in the film and on the soundtrack album
Space Jam (Warner Sunset/Atlantic, 97).

455 Rocket
Words and music by Gillian Welsh and David Rawlings.
Irving Music Inc., 1997/Crack Music, 1997/Bug Music, 1997.
Best-selling record by Kathy Mattea from the album *Love Travels*
(Mercury, 97).

Four Leaf Clover
Words and music by Abra Moore.
Abra Songs, 1997/Maverick, 1997/WB Music, 1997.
Introduced by Abra Moore on the album *Strangest Places* (Arista Texas,
97).

4 Seasons of Loneliness
Words and music by James Harris, III and Terry Lewis.
EMI-April Music, 1997/Flyte Tyme Tunes, 1997.
Best-selling record by Boyz II Men from the album *Evolution* (Motown, 97).

Fourth of July
Words and music by Dave Alvin.
Blue Horn Toad, 1987/Bug Music, 1987.
Revived by Robert Earl Keen on the album *Picnic* (Arista Austin, 97).

4th of July, Asbury Park (Sandy)
Words and music by Bruce Springsteen.
Bruce Springsteen Publishing, 1972.
Revived by Ben E. King on the album *One Step Up/One Step Back--The Songs of Bruce Springsteen* (The Right Stuff, 97).

Freaks
Words and music by Live.
Loco De Amor, New York, 1997/Audible Sun, New York, 1997.
Best-selling record by Live from the album *Secret Samadhi* (MCA, 97).

Free to Decide (Irish)
Words and music by Delores O'Riordan.
Polygram International Music, 1996.
Best-selling record by The Cranberries from the album *To the Faithful Departed* (Island, 96).

Freedom
Words and music by Madonna Ciccone and Dallas Austin.
Webo Girl, 1997/WB Music, 1997/EMI-April Music, 1997/D.A.R.P. Music, 1997.
Introduced by Madonna on the album *Carnival* (RCA, 97).

The Freshmen
Words and music by Brian Vander Ark.
Sid Flips Music, 1994/EMI-April Music, 1994.
Best-selling record by the Verve Pipe from the album *Villains* (RCA, 97).

The Friends
Words and music by Jerry Holland.
Mike Curb Productions, 1996/That's a Smash Music, 1996.
Best-selling record by John Michael Montgomery from the album *What I Do Best* (Atlantic, 96).

From Here to Eternity
Words and music by Michael Peterson and Robert Ellis Orrall.
Warner-Tamerlane Music, 1997/EMI-April Music, 1997/Kids Music,

1997.
Best-selling record by Michael Peterson from the album *Michael Peterson* (Reprise, 97).

G

Gangstas Make the World Go Round
Words and music by Ice Cube (pseudonym for O'Shea Jackson), Dedric
   Rolison, William Calhoun, Cedric Samson, Thom Bell, and Linda
   Creed.
Gangsta Boogie, 1996/WB Music, 1996/Real an Ruff Music, 1996/Base
   Pipe Music, 1996/Warner-Tamerlane Music, 1996.
Best-selling record by Westside Connection from the album *Bow Down*
   (Priority, 96).

The Gentleman Is a Dope
Words and music by Oscar Hammerstein, II and Richard Rodgers.
Williamson Music, 1947.
Revived by Barbara Cook on the album *Oscar Winners--The Lyrics of
   Oscar Hammerstein II* (DRG, 97). Originally introduced by Lisa Kirk
   in the musical *Allegro*.

Get It Together
Words and music by Donell Jones.
Check Man Music, 1997/Ness, Nitty & Capone, 1997/Warner-Chappell
   Music, 1997.
Best-selling record by 702 from the album *No Doubt* (Motown, 97).

Ghetto Love
Words and music by Da Brat (pseudonym for Shawntae Harris), Eldra
   DeBarge, Carlton Riddenhour, and James Boxley, III.
Zomba Music, 1996/BDP Music, 1996/Jobete Music Co., 1996/Bring the
   Noize Music, 1996/So So Def American Music, 1996.
Best-selling record by Da Brat Featuring T-Boz from the album
   Anuthatantrum (Columbia, 97).

G.H.E.T.T.O.U.T.
Words and music by Robert Kelly.
Zomba Music, 1997/R. Kelly Music, 1997.
Best-selling record by Changing Faces from the album *All Day, All
   Night* (Atlantic, 97).

The Girl I Love She Got Long Black Wavy Hair
Words and music by Sleepy John Estes.
MCA/Northern Music, Los Angeles, 1930.
Reissued by Led Zeppelin on the album *The BBC Sessions* (Atlantic, 97). Recorded for the British radio show, *Tasty Pop Sundae*, circa 1970.

A Girl's Gotta Do What a Girl's Gotta Do
Words and music by Rick Bowles and Rick Byrne.
Maypop Music, 1996/Wildcountry, 1996/Makin' Chevys Music, 1996/ EMI-Blackwood Music Inc., 1996/Artbyme Music, 1996/Mike Curb Productions, 1996/Diamond Storm Music, 1996.
Best-selling record by Mindy McCready from the album *10,000 Angels* (BNA, 96).

Go Away
Words and music by Stephony Smith, Cathy Majeski, and Sunny Russ.
EMI-Blackwood Music Inc., 1997/Starstruck Angel Music, 1997/Sony ATV Cross Keys Publishing Co. Inc., 1997/All Around Town Music, 1997.
Best-selling record by Lorrie Morgan from the album *Shakin' Things Up* (BNA, 97).

Go the Distance
Words and music by David Zippel and Alan Menken.
Walt Disney Music, 1997/Wonderland Music, 1997.
Best-selling record by Michael Bolton in the film and on the soundtrack album *Hercules* (Columbia, 97). Nominated for an Academy Award, Best Song of the Year, 1997.

Godspeed Titanic
Words and music by Maury Yeston.
Yeston Music, Ltd., 1997.
Introduced by the chorus in the musical and on the cast album *Titanic* (RCA Victor, 97).

Gone Away
Words and music by Bryan Keith Hubbard.
Underachiever Music, Calabasas, 1997.
Best-selling record by the Offspring from the album *Ixnay on the Hombre* (Columbia, 97).

Good as I Was to You
Words and music by Don Schlitz and Billy Livsey.
New Don Music, 1997/New Hayes Music, 1997/Rondo Music, 1997/ Irving Music Inc., 1997.
Best-selling record by Lorrie Morgan from the album *Shakin' Things Up* (BNA, 97).

Good Night Elizabeth
Words and music by Adam Duritz.
EMI-Blackwood Music Inc., 1996/Island Music, 1996.
Best-selling record by Counting Crows from the album *Recovering the Satellites* (Geffen, 96).

Good Riddance (Time of Your Life)
Words and music by Billie Joe Armstrong and Green Day.
WB Music, 1997/Green Daze, 1997.
Best-selling record by Green Day from the album *Nimrod* (Reprise, 97).

Good Time Charlie's Got the Blues
Words and music by Danny O'Keefe.
Warner-Tamerlane Music, 1968.
Revived by Dwight Yoakam on the album *Under the Covers* (Reprise, 97).

Got Till It's Gone
Words and music by Rene Elizando, Kamaal Ibn Fareed, Janet Jackson, James Harris, III, Terry Lewis, and Joni Mitchell.
Black Ice Music, 1997/Flyte Tyme Tunes, 1997/Siquomb Publishing Corp., 1997/Sony ATV Music, 1997/Jazz Merchant Music, 1997/Zomba Music, 1997.
Best-selling record by Janet Jackson from the album *Velvet Rope* (Virgin, 97). This song makes use of Joni Mitchell's "Big Yellow Taxi."

Gotham City (Theme from *Batman and Robin*)
Words and music by Robert Kelly.
Zomba Music, 1997/R. Kelly Music, 1997.
Best-selling record by R. Kelly in the film and on the soundtrack album *Batman and Robin* (Warner Sunset/Warner Brothers, 97).

The Great American Nightmare
Words and music by Rob Zombie and Charlie Clouser.
WB Music, 1997/Rysher Music, 1997/Demenoid Deluxe Music, 1997/ControlMusic, 1997/Rysher Songs.
Introduced by Rob Zombie and Howard Stern in the film and on the soundtrack album *Howard Stern's Private Parts* (Warner Brothers, 97).

Greedy Fly (English)
Words and music by Gavin Rossdale.
Warner-Tamerlane Music, 1997/Truly Soothing Elevator Music, 1997/Mad Dog Winston Music.
Best-selling record by Bush from the album *Razorblade Suitcase* (Interscope, 97).

Guantanamera
Words and music by Pete Seeger and Jose Marti.
Fall River Music Inc., 1968.
Revived by Wyclef Jean with Lauryn Hill, Kamani Marley, Celia Cruz,
    and Beenie Man on the album *Carnival* (Ruffhouse/Columbia, 97).
    This is an update of Pete Seeger's Latin American freedom-fighting
    anthem.

H

Half Way Up
Words and music by Clint Black and Hayden Nicholas.
Blackened Music, 1996.
Best-selling record by Clint Black from the album *Clint Black--Greatest Hits* (RCA, 96).

Hard to Say I'm Sorry (American-Canadian)
Words and music by Peter Cetera and David Foster.
Double Virgo Music, 1997/Foster Frees Music Inc., 1997.
Revived by Az Yet on the album *Az Yet* (LaFace, 96).

Head over Heels
Words and music by Mariah Carey, Nasir Jones, Samuel Barnes, Jean Claude Olivier, Marlon Williams, and Shawn Moltke.
American Romance Music, Nashville, 1997/Sony ATV Songs, 1997/Rye Songs, 1997/I'll Will, 1997/Zomba Music, 1997/Slam U Well Music, 1997/Jelly's Jams L.L.C. Music, 1997/Jumping Bean Music, 1997.
Best-selling record by Allure featuring NAS from the album *Allure* (Crave, 97).

Heaven
Words and music by Rico Luna, Frank Pangelinan, and Jacob Ceniceros.
O.C.D. Music, Palmdale, 1997.
Best-selling record by Nu Flavor from the album *Nu Flavor* (Reprise, 97).

Hell
Words and music by Tom Maxwell and Jim Mathus.
Bughouse, 1997.
Best-selling record by Squirrel Nut Zippers from the album *Hot* (Mammoth, 97). It portrayed Hell as a retro lounge.

Here in My Heart
Words and music by Glen Ballard and James Newton Howard.
Famous Music Corp., 1997/MCA Music, 1997.

31

Best-selling record by Chicago from the album *The Heart of Chicago 1967--1997* (Reprise, 97).

He's Got You
Words and music by Ronnie Dunn and Jim McBride.
Sony ATV Tree Publishing, 1997/Showbilly, 1997/Warner-Tamerlane Music, 1997/Constant Pressure Music, 1997.
Best-selling record by Brooks & Dunn from the album *Brooks & Dunn--The Greatest Hits Collection* (Arista Nashville, 97).

Hey Girl
Words and music by Gerry Goffin and Carole King.
Screen Gems-EMI Music Inc., 1963.
Revived by Billy Joel on the album *Billy Joel--Greatest Hits, Volume 3* (Columbia, 97). This was popularized by Freddy Scott.

Highlands
Words and music by Bob Dylan.
Special Rider Music, 1997.
Introduced by Bob Dylan on the album *Time out of Mind* (Columbia, 97). At age 56, Dylan proved that he was still capable of producing a 16-minute song.

Holdin'
Words and music by Kelly Garrett and Craig Wiseman.
Irving Music Inc., 1997/Kelly Garrett Music, 1997/Almo Music Corp., 1997/Daddy Rabbitt Music, 1997/Sony ATV Tree Publishing, 1997.
Best-selling record by Diamond Rio from the album *Diamond Rio--Greatest Hits* (Arista, 97).

Hole in My Soul
Words and music by Steven Tyler, Joe Perry, and Desmond Child.
Swag Song Music, 1997/EMI-April Music, 1997/Desmobile Music Inc., 1997.
Best-selling record by Aerosmith from the album *Nine Lives* (Columbia, 97).

Honey
Words and music by Mariah Carey, Sean "Puffy" Combs, Kamaal Ibn Fareed, Steve Jordan, S. Hague, Bobby Robinson, R. Larkins, and Kelly Price.
Sony ATV Songs, 1997/Rye Songs, 1997/Justin Combs Music, 1997/ EMI-April Music, 1997/Zomba Music, 1997/Jazz Merchant Music, 1997/Steven A. Jordan Music, 1997/Bobby Robinson Music, 1997.
Best-selling record by Mariah Carey from the album *Butterfly* (Columbia, 97). Nominated for a Grammy Award, Best R&B Song of the Year, 1997.

Honky Tonk Truth
Words and music by Kix Dunn, Kim Williams, and Lonnie Wilson.
Sony ATV Tree Publishing, 1997/Showbilly, 1997/Sony ATV Cross
   Keys Publishing Co. Inc., 1997/Kim Williams, 1997/Zomba Music,
   1997.
Best-selling record by Brooks & Dunn from the album *Brooks & Dunn-
   -The Greatest Hits Collection* (Arista Nashville, 97).

How Bizarre (New Zealand)
Words and music by Pauly Fuemana and Alan Jansson.
Songs of Polygram, 1997.
Best-selling record by OMC from the album *How Bizzare* (Huh/
   Mercury, 97). It was this year's most cinematic lyric for whoever
   "buys the rights."

How Come, How Long
Words and music by Babyface (pseudonym for Kenny Edmunds) and
   Stevie Wonder.
Steveland Music, Burbank, 1996/Sony ATV Songs, 1996/Ecaf Music,
   1996.
Introduced by Babyface and Stevie Wonder on the album *The Day*
   (Epic, 96). The meeting of the titans. It is also featured on the album
   MTV Unplugged in NYC.

How a Cowgirl Says Goodbye
Words and music by Larry Boone, Pete Nelson, and Tracy Lawrence.
Sony ATV Cross Keys Publishing Co. Inc., 1997/Sony ATV Tree
   Publishing, 1997/SLL Music, 1997/Terilee Music, 1997.
Best-selling record by Tracy Lawrence from the album *The Coast Is
   Clear* (Atlantic, 97).

How Do I Get There
Words and music by Deana Carter and Chris Farren.
Farrenuff, 1996/Full Keel Music, 1996/EMI-Princeton Street Music,
   1996.
Best-selling record by Deana Carter from the album *Did I Shave My
   Legs for This* (Capitol Nashville, 96).

How Do I Live
Words and music by Diane Warren.
Realsongs, 1997.
Introduced by Trisha Yearwood in the film and on the soundtrack album
   Con Air (MCA, 97). Best-selling record by LeAnn Rimes from the
   album *You Light Up My Life* (Curb, 97). Nominated for an Academy
   Award, Best Song of the Year, 1997; Nominated for an Academy
   Award, Best Song of the Year, 1997; a Grammy Award, Best Song of
   the Year, 1997.

How Was I to Know
Words and music by Eric Blair Daly and William Rambeaux.
Reynsong Music, 1997/Bayou Bay Music, 1997/Kentucky Girl Music, 1997.
Best-selling record by John Michael Montgomery from the album *What I Do Best* (Atlantic, 97).

How Was I to Know
Words and music by Cathy Majeski, Sunny Russ, and Stephony Smith.
Sony ATV Cross Keys Publishing Co. Inc., 1996/All Around Town Music, 1996/Starstruck Angel Music, 1996/EMI-Blackwood Music Inc., 1996.
Best-selling record by Reba McEntire from the album *What's It to You* (MCA, 96).

How Your Love Makes Me Feel
Words and music by Max T. Barnes and Trey Bruce.
Island Bound Music, 1997/Famous Music Corp., 1997/Pop a Wheelie Music, 1997/Big Tractor Music, 1997/WB Music, 1997.
Best-selling record by Diamond Rio from the album *Diamond Rio-- Greatest Hits* (Arista Nashville, 97).

How's It Gonna Be
Words and music by Stephan Jenkins and Kevin Cadogan.
3EB Music, 1997/Caddagh Hill Music, 1997.
Best-selling record by Third Eye Blind from the album *Third Eye Blind* (Elektra, 97).

Hush
Words and music by Joe South.
Lowery Music Co., Inc., 1967.
Revived by Kula Shaker in the film and on the soundtrack album *I Know What You Did Last Summer* (Columbia, 97). Joe South and Deep Purple had hits with this song.

Hypnotize
Words and music by Christopher Wallace, Sean "Puffy" Combs, Derek Angelettie, Ronald Lawrence, Andy Armer, and Randy Alpert.
Big Poppa Music, 1997/Justin Combs Music, 1997/EMI-April Music, 1997/Mystery System Music, 1997/Almo Music Corp., 1997/Badazz Music, 1997/Danica Music, 1997/Entertaining Music, 1997.
Best-selling record by The Notorious B.I.G. from the album *Life After Death* (Arista, 97).

I

I Believe I Can Fly
Words and music by Robert Kelly.
Zomba Music, 1996/R. Kelly Music, 1996.
Best-selling record by R. Kelly in the film and on the soundtrack album *Space Jam* (Jive, 96). Nominated for Grammy Awards, Best R&B Song of the Year, 1997, Best Record of the Year, 1997 and Best Song of the Year, 1997.

I Believe in You and Me
Words and music by David Wolfert and Sandy Linzer.
Charles Koppelman Music, 1997/Martin Bandier Music, 1997/Jonathan Three Music Co., 1997/Linzer Music, 1997.
Best-selling record by Whitney Houston in the film and on the soundtrack album *The Preacher's Wife* (Arista, 97).

I Belong to You (Everytime I See Your Face)
Words and music by Gerald Baillergeau.
Mike's Rap Music, Valencia, 1997.
Best-selling record by Rome from the album *Rome* (RCA, 97).

I Can Love You
Words and music by Mary J. Blige, Latonya Blige-Decosta, Rodney Jerkins, Kim Jones, Carlos Brody, and Nashiel Myrick.
MCA Music, 1997/Mary J. Blige, 1997/EMI-Blackwood Music Inc., 1997/Rodney Jerkins Music, 1997/Undeas Music, 1997/Warner-Tamerlane Music, 1997/6th of July Music, 1997/NASHMACK Music, 1997.
Best-selling record by Mary J. Blige from the album *Share My World* (MCA, 97).

I Can't Do That Anymore
Words and music by Alan Jackson.
Yee Haw Music, Nashville, 1996/WB Music, 1996.
Best-selling record by Faith Hill from the album *It Matters to Me* (Warner Brothers, 96).

I Can't Read (English)
Words and music by David Bowie.
Tintoretto Music, 1989.
Revived by David Bowie in the film and on the soundtrack album *The Ice Storm* (Real Sounds/Velvel, 97). The song was reinterpreted for the film.

I Care 'Bout You
Words and music by Babyface (pseudonym for Kenny Edmunds).
Sony ATV Songs, 1997/Ecaf Music, 1997/Fox Film Music Corp., 1997.
Best-selling record by Milestone in the film and on the soundtrack album *Soul Food* (Laface/Arista, 97).

I Choose
Words and music by Bryan Keith Hubbard.
Underachiever Music, Calabasas, 1997.
Best-selling record by The Offspring from the album *Ixnay on the Hombre* (Columbia, 97).

I Do
Words and music by Lisa Loeb.
Furious Rose, New York, 1997/Music Corp. of America, 1997.
Best-selling record by Lisa Loeb from the album *Firecracker* (Geffen, 97).

I Don't Ever Want to See You Again
Words and music by Nathan Morris.
Vanderpool Music, 1997/Ensign Music, 1997.
Best-selling record by Uncle Sam from the album *Uncle Sam* (Stonecreek/Epic, 97).

I Don't Want To
Words and music by Robert Kelly.
R. Kelly Music, 1997/Zomba Music, 1997.
Best-selling record by Toni Braxton from the album *Secrets* (LaFace/Arista, 97).

I Don't Want to Wait
Words and music by Paula Cole.
Hingface Music, 1997/Ensign Music, 1997.
Best-selling record by Paula Cole from the album *This Fire* (Warner Brothers, 97).

I Left Something Turned on at Home
Words and music by Billy Lawson and John Schweers.
Castle Street, Nashville, 1997/Catch the Boat Music, Nashville, 1997.
Best-selling record by Trace Adkins from the album *Big Time* (Capitol Nashville, 97).

I Like It (Like That)
Words and music by Manny Rodriguez and Tony Pabon.
Longitude Music, 1994.
Revived by by the Blackout Allstars in a TV commercial for Burger
    King. It was also on the album *AVP Summer Soundtrack* (Columbia,
    97).

I Love L.A.
Words and music by Randy Newman.
Randy Newman Music, 1983.
Revived by OMC in the film and on the soundtrack album *Bean*
    (Mercury, 97).

I Love Me Some Him
Words and music by Andrea Martin, Gloria Stewart, Soulshock, and
    Kenneth Karlin.
EMI Music Publishing, 1997/Casadida, 1997/Salandra Music, 1997/
    Almo Music Corp., 1997/Plaything Music, 1997/Too True Music,
    1997.
Best-selling record by Toni Braxton from the album *Secrets* (Arista, 96).

I Miss My Homies
Words and music by Master P, Pimp C, and The Shocker.
Burrin Avenue Music, Hollywood, 1997/Big P Music, Baton Rouge,
    1997.
Best-selling record by Master P featuring Pimp C and The Shocker from
    the album *Ghetto D* (Priority, 97).

I Miss You a Little
Words and music by Mike Anthony, Richard Fagan, and John Michael
    Montgomery.
Hot Hooks Music, 1996/JMM Music, 1996/Of Music, 1996.
Best-selling record by John Michael Montgomery from the album *What
    I Do Best* (Atlantic, 96).

I Only Get This Way with You
Words and music by Dave Loggins and Alan Ray.
MCA Music, 1997.
Best-selling record by Rick Trevino from the album *Learning as You
    Go* (Columbia, 97).

I Say a Little Prayer
Words and music by Burt Bacharach and Hal David.
New Hidden Valley Music Co., 1967/Casa David, 1967.
Revived by the cast of the movie *My Best Friend's Wedding* (Work/
    Sony Music Soundtrax, 97). Also revived by Diana King on the
    album *My Best Friend's Wedding* (Work Group, 97). Arguably the
    best song usage of the year.

I Shot the Sheriff (American-Jamaican)
Words and music by Bob Marley, Lawrence Parker, Tony C., Erick
  Sermon, and Pete Smith.
Zomba Music, 1974/House of Fun Music, 1974/337 LLC Music, 1974/
  Cayman Music.
Revived by Warren G. on the album *Take a Look over Your Shoulder*
  (Mercury, 97). This is a rewrite of the Bob Marley classic.

I Turn to You
Words and music by Diane Warren.
Realsongs, 1996/WB Music, 1996.
Introduced by All-4-One in the film and on the soundtrack album *Space
  Jam* (Warner Sunset/Atlantic, 96). Also on the album *My Brother's
  Keeper* (Blitzz/Warner Sunset/Atlantic, 97).

I Wanna Be There
Words and music by Elliot Sloan, Jeff Pence, Emosia, and Eddie
  Hedges.
EMI-April Music, 1997/Tosha Music, 1997/Shapiro, Bernstein & Co.,
  Inc., 1997.
Best-selling record by Blessid Union of Souls from the album *Blessid
  Union of Souls* (EMI, 97).

I Want You (Australian)
Words and music by Darren Hayes and Damon Jones.
EMI-Blackwood Music Inc., 1997/EMI Music Publishing, 1997/Rough
  Cut Music, 1997.
Best-selling record by Savage Garden from the album *Savage Garden*
  (Columbia, 97).

I Was Born in Puerto Rico
Words and music by Paul Simon and Derek Walcott.
Paul Simon Music, 1997.
Introduced by Paul Simon on the album *Songs from the Capeman*
  (Warner Brothers, 97). This was also introduced by Ruben Blades in
  the musical *The Capeman*.

I Will Be Loved
Words and music by Joe DiPietro and Jimmy Roberts.
Introduced by Jennifer Simard in the musical revue and on the cast
  album *I Love You, You're Perfect, Now Change* (Varese Sarabande,
  97).

I Will Come to You
Words and music by Issac Hanson, Zac Hanson, Taylor Hanson, Barry
  Mann, and Cynthia Weil.
Jam N' Bread Music, 1997/Heavy Harmony Music, 1997/Dyad Music,
  Ltd., 1997/MCA Music, 1997/Beef Puppet.

Best-selling record by Hanson from the album *Middle of Nowhere* (Mercury, 97).

I Wish I Knew How It Would Feel to Be Free
Words and music by Billy Taylor and Dick Dallas.
Duane Music, Inc., 1964.
Revived by Dionne Farris in the film and on the soundtrack album *Ghosts of Mississippi* (Columbia, 97). Also revived by Nina Simone on the soundtrack album *Ghosts of Mississippi* (Columbia, 97). This was initially popularized by Simone.

I'd Rather Ride Around with You
Words and music by Mark D. Sanders and Tim Nichols.
Mark D. Music, 1996/Tyland Music, 1996/Starstruck Writers Group, 1996/EMI Blackwood Music Inc.
Best-selling record by Reba McEntire from the album *What's It to You* (MCA, 96).

If I Could Teach the World
Words and music by Bone and D. J. U-Neek.
Ruthless Attack Muzick, 1997/Mo Thug Music, 1997/Keeno Music, 1997.
Best-selling record by Bone Thugs-N-Harmony from the album *The Art of War* (Relativity, 97).

If She Don't Love You
Words and music by Trey Bruce and Mark Beeson.
WB Music, 1997/Big Tractor Music, 1997/EMI-April Music, 1997/K-Town Music, 1997.
Best-selling record by The Buffalo Club from the album *The Buffalo Club* (Rising Tide, 97).

If We Fall in Love Tonight
Words and music by James Harris, III and Terry Lewis.
EMI-April Music, 1996/Flyte Tyme Tunes, 1996.
Best-selling record by Rod Stewart from the album *If We Fall in Love Tonight* (Warner Brothers, 97).

If You Could Only See
Words and music by Emerson Hart.
EMI-Blackwood Music Inc., 1997/Crazy Owl Music, 1997/Unconcerned Music.
Best-selling record by Tonic from the album *Lemon Parade* (A & M, 97).

If You Love Somebody
Words and music by Chris Farren and Jeffrey Steele.
Farrenuff, 1997/Full Keel Music, 1997/Longitude Music, 1997/Blue Desert Music, 1997.

Best-selling record by Kevin Sharp from the album *Measure of a Man* (Asylum, 97).

I'll Always Be Right There (American-Canadian)
Words and music by Bryan Adams, Robert John "Mutt" Lange, and Michael Kamen.
Badams Music, 1996/Zomba Music, 1996/K-Man.
Best-selling record by Bryan Adams from the album *18 Till I Die* (A & M, 96).

I'll Be
Words and music by Sean Carter, Jean Claude Olivier, Samuel Barnes, Angela Winbush, and Rene Moore.
Slam U Well Music, 1997/Jelly's Jams L.L.C. Music, 1997/Twelve & Under Music, 1997/Jumping Bean Music, 1997/Lil Lu Lu Music, 1997/A La Mode Music, 1997.
Best-selling record by Foxy Brown featuring Jay-Z from the album *Ill Na Na* (Mercury, 97).

I'll Be Missing You (American-English)
Words and music by Sting (pseudonym for Gordon Sumner), Todd Gaither, and Faith Evans.
Magnetic Music Publishing Co., 1997/Blue Turtle, 1997/Illegal Songs, Inc., 1997/September Six Music, 1997/Chyna Baby Music, 1997/Janice Combs Music, 1997/EMI-Blackwood Music Inc., 1997.
Best-selling record by Puff Daddy and Faith Evans from the album *NoWay Out* (Arista, 97). This is a tribute and eulogy to Christopher Wallace, a.k.a. The Notorious B.I.G., with help from "Every Breath You Take" by The Police.

I'll Never Fall in Love Again
Words and music by Burt Bacharach and Hal David.
New Hidden Valley Music Co., 1968/Casa David, 1968.
Revived by Mary Chapin Carpenter in the film and on the soundtrack album *My Best Friend's Wedding* (Work/Sony Music Soundtrack, 97). This film ignited this year's brief Bacharach mania.

I'm Not Giving You Up
Words and music by Gloria Estefan and Flavio Santander.
Foreign Imported, 1997.
Best-selling record by Gloria Estefan from the album *Destiny* (Epic, 97).

I'm So Happy I Can't Stop Crying (American-English)
Words and music by Sting (pseudonym for Gordon Sumner).
Magnetic Music Publishing Co., 1996/Regatta Music, Ltd., 1996/Illegal Songs, Inc., 1996.
Revived by by Toby Keith with Sting from the album *Dream Walkin'*

(Mercury, 97). Introduced by Sting on the album *Mercury Falling* (A & M, 96).

I'm Thru with Love
Words and music by Gus Kahn, Matt Malneck, and Fud Livingston. Robbins Music Corp., 1931.
Revived by Goldie Hawn and Woody Allen in the film and on the soundtrack album *Everyone Says I Love You* (RCA Victor, 97).

Impossible
Words and music by Richard Rodgers and Oscar Hammerstein, II. Williamson Music, 1957.
Revived by Whitney Houston on the TV special *Rodgers & Hammerstein's Cinderella*.

The Impression That I Get
Words and music by Dicky Barrett and Joe Gittleman. Famous Music Corp., 1997/EMI-April Music, 1997.
Best-selling record by The Mighty Mighty Bosstones from the album *Let's Face It* (Big Rig/Mercury, 97).

In Another's Eyes
Words and music by Bobby Wood, John Peppard, and Garth Brooks. Major Bob Music, 1997/No Fences Music, 1997/Rio Bravo Music, 1997/Cat's Eye Music, 1997.
Best-selling record by Trisha Yearwood and Garth Brooks from the album *Songbook (A Collection of Hits)* (MCA, 97). Nominated for a Grammy Award, Best Country Song of the Year, 1997.

In the Jailhouse Now
Words and music by Jimmie Rodgers. Peer International Corp., 1928.
Revived by Steve Earle on the album *The Songs of Jimmie Rodgers--A Tribute* (Egyptian/Columbia, 97).

In My Bed
Words and music by Rafael Brown, Ralph Stacy, and Darryl Simmons. Brown Lace, 1996/Zomba Music, 1996/Stacegoo Music, 1996/Warner-Tamerlane Music, 1996/Boobie-Loo, 1996.
Best-selling record by Dru Hill from the album *Dru Hill* (Island, 96).

Invisible Man
Words and music by Dane Deviller, Sean Hosein, and Steve Kipner. Banana Tunes Music, 1997/Stephen A. Kipner Music, 1997/Careers-BMG Music, 1997/Bubalas, 1997/On Board Music, 1997.
Best-selling record by 98 Degrees from the album *98 Degrees* (Motown, 97).

Is All of This for Me
Words and music by Henry Gross and Roger Cook.
Half Mine Music, 1997/EMI-Blackwood Music Inc., 1997/Song Island
   Music, 1997/Golly Rogers Music, 1997.
Introduced by Tracy Nelson on the album *Scotty Moore and DJ
   Fontana--All the King's Men* (Sweetfish, 97).

Is That a Tear
Words and music by John Jarrard and Ken Beard.
Alabama Band Music Co., 1997/Wildcountry, 1997/Lac Grand Music,
   1997/Miss Blyss Music, 1997.
Best-selling record by Tracy Lawrence from the album *The Coast Is
   Clear* (Atlantic, 97).

It's All About the Benjamins
Words and music by Jacobs, Phillips, Styles, Christopher Wallace, Kim
   Jones, Sean "Puffy" Combs, Derek Angelettie, David Bowie, and Eric
   Blackmon.
Sheek Louchion Music, 1997/Jae'wans Music, 1997/Paniro's Music,
   1997/Big Poppa Music, 1997/Justin Combs Music, 1997/EMI-April
   Music, 1997/Undeas Music, 1997/Crazy Cat Catalogue, 1997/Funky
   Stix Music, 1997.
Best-selling record by Puff Daddy & the Family from the album *No
   Way Out* (Bad Boy/Arista, 97).

It's Hard to Be a Saint in the City
Words and music by Bruce Springsteen.
Bruce Springsteen Publishing, 1972.
Revived by David Bowie on the album *One Step Up/One Step Back--
   The Songs of Bruce Springsteen* (The Right Stuff, 97).

It's a Little Too Late
Words and music by Mark Chesnutt, Clessie Lee Morrisette, and Roger
   Springer.
EMI-Blackwood Music Inc., 1996/Songs of Jasper, 1996/The Fat Rat
   Music, 1996/EMI-April Music, 1996/WB Music, 1996.
Best-selling record by Mark Chesnutt from the album *Mark Chesnutt--
   Greatest Hits* (Decca, 97).

It's No Good (English)
Words and music by Martin Gore.
EMI Music Publishing, 1997/EMI-Blackwood Music Inc., 1997.
Best-selling record by Depeche Mode from the album *Ultra* (Reprise,
   97).

It's Raining Men--The Sequel
Words and music by Paul Jabara and Paul Shaffer.
Olga Music, 1981/Jonathan Three Music Co., 1981/EMI-Josaha Music,

1981.

Revived by Martha Wash and Rupaul on the album *The Collection* (Logic, 97). Wash's previous version was with the Weather Girls.

It's Your Love

Words and music by Stephony Smith.

EMI-Blackwood Music Inc., 1997.

Best-selling record by Tim McGraw (with Faith Hill) from the album *Everywhere* (Curb, 97). Nominated for a Grammy Award, Best Country Song of the Year, 1997.

J

Jessie's Girl (Australian)
Words and music by Rick Springfield.
Songs of Polygram, 1981.
Revived by Rick Springfield in the film and on the soundtrack album
   Boogie Nights (Capitol, 97).

Jesus, the Missing Years
Words and music by John Prine.
Weowna Music, 1991/Bug Music, 1991.
Revived by John Prine on the album *Live on Tour* (Oh Boy, 97). Prine
   received a Grammy nomination for this album.

Joga (Swedish)
English words and music by Bjork Gudmundsdottir and Sugurjon Birgir
   Sigurdsson.
F.S. Ltd., England, 1997/Peer Music, 1997/SPZ, 1997.
Introduced by Bjork on the album *Homegenic* (Elektra, 97).

Journey to the Past
Words and music by Stephen Flaherty and Lynn Ahrens.
TCF Music, 1997.
Introduced by Aaliyah in the film and on the soundtrack album
   Anastasia (Atlantic, 97). Nominated for an Academy Award, Best
   Song of the Year, 1997.

Jungle
Words and music by Paul Stanley, Bruce Kulick, and Cuomo.
Hori Pro America, 1997/Polygram Music Publishing Inc., 1997.
Best-selling record by Kiss from the album *Carnival of Souls--The Final
   Sessions* (Mercury, 97).

L

Lakini's Juice
Words and music by Live.
Loco De Amor, New York, 1997/Audible Sun, New York, 1997.
Best-selling record by Live from the album *Secret Samadhi* (MCA, 97).

Land of the Living
Words and music by Wayland Patton and Tia Sillers.
MCA Music, 1997/Delta Kappa Twang Music, 1997/Tom Collins Music
Corp., 1997.
Best-selling record by Pam Tillis from the album *Pam Tillis--Greatest
Hits* (Arista Nashville, 97).

Laughing Matters
Words and music by Dick Gallagher.
Introduced by Jay Rogers in the musical and on the cast album *When
Pigs Fly* (RCA, 97). This was also recorded by Karen Akers on the
album *Live at the Rainbow and Stars* (DRG, 97). Bette Midler has a
version of this song due out in '98.

Legend of a Cowgirl (American-English)
Words and music by Imani Coppola, Donovan Leitch, and Michael
Mangini.
Donovan Music, Ltd., London, England, 1997/Tsanoddnos Music, 1997/
Ensign Music, 1997/Ash Belle Music, 1997/Gee Street Music, 1997/
Famous Music Corp., 1997/Peer International Corp., 1997.
Best-selling record by Imani Coppola from the album *Chupacabra*
(Columbia, 97).

Let Down (English)
Words and music by Colin Greenwood, Johnny Greenwood, Ed
O'Brien, Phil Selway, and Thom Yorke.
Warner-Chappell Music, 1997.
Introduced by Radiohead on the album *OK Computer* (Capitol, 97).

Let It Go
Words and music by Keith Crouch, Glenn McKinney, and Roy Pennon.
Human Rhythm, 1997/Daaa!!! Music, 1997/Fat Hat Music, 1997.
Best-selling record by Ray J in the film and on the soundtrack album
    Set It Off (EEG, 97).

Let It Rain
Words and music by Mark Chesnutt, Steve Leslie, and Roger Springer.
EMI-Blackwood Music Inc., 1997/EMI-April Music, 1997/Songs of
    Jasper, 1997.
Best-selling record by Mark Chesnutt from the album *Mark Chesnutt--*
    Greatest Hits (Decca, 97).

Let Me Clear My Throat
Words and music by DJ Kool.
Kool Music, 1997/CLR Music, 1997/WB Music, 1997.
Best-selling record by DJ Kool from the album *Let Me Clear My Throat*
    (Warner Brothers, 97).

Let's Kill Saturday Night
Words and music by Robbie Fulks.
Songwriters Ink, 1997.
Introduced by The Five Chinese Brothers on the album *Let's Kill*
    Saturday Night (1-800-Prime CD, 97).

Lie to Me
Words and music by Bruce McCabe and David Z.
Ryan Cory Music, Minneapolis, 1997/David Z Music, Hollywood, 1997.
Best-selling record by Johnny Lang from the album *Lie to Me* (A & M,
    97).

The Life
Words and music by Cy Coleman and Ira Gasman.
Notable Music Co., Inc., 1996/Chappell & Co., Inc., 1996.
Introduced by Pamela Isaacs in the musical and on the cast album *The*
    Life (RCA, 97).

The Light in Your Eyes
Words and music by Daniel Tyler.
Mota Music, 1997.
Best-selling record by LeAnn Rimes from the album *You Light Up My*
    Life (Curb, 97).

Line Em Up
Words and music by James Taylor.
Country Road Music Inc., 1997.
Introduced by James Taylor on the album *Hourglass* (Columbia, 97).

Listen
Words and music by Ed Roland.
Sugarbuzz Music, 1997/Warner-Chappell Music, 1997.
Best-selling record by Collective Soul from the album *Disciplined Breakdown* (Atlantic, 97).

A Little More Love
Words and music by Vince Gill.
Benefit Music, 1996.
Best-selling record by Vince Gill from the album *High Lonesome Sound* (MCA, 96).

Little More Time with You
Words and music by James Taylor.
Country Road Music, Los Angeles, 1997.
Best-selling record by James Taylor from the album *Hourglass* (Columbia, 97).

Little Things
Words and music by Michael Dulaney and Steven Dale Jones.
Ensign Music, 1997/Island Bound Music, 1997/Famous Music Corp.
Best-selling record by Tanya Tucker from the album *Complicated* (Capitol Nashville, 97).

Little White Lie
Words and music by Sammy Hagar.
WB Music, 1997/The Nine Music, 1997.
Best-selling record by Sammy Hagar from the album *Marching to Mars* (MCA, 97).

Live as You Dream (English)
Words and music by Beth Orton, Ted Barnes, and Alistair Friend.
EMI-Blackwood Music Inc., 1997/Virgin Music, 1997.
Introduced by Beth Orton on the album *Trailer Park* (Dedicated, 97).

Living for the City
Words and music by Stevie Wonder.
Jobete Music Co., 1973/Black Bull Music, 1973.
Revived by Ray Charles on the album *Genius + Soul--The 50th Anniversary Collection* (Rhino, 97). Also revived by Zapp & Roger on the album *The Compilation: Greatest Hits II* (Reprise, 96).

Lollipop (Candyman) (Danish)
English words and music by Soren Rasted, Claus Noreen, and Lene Grawford Nystrom.
MCA Music, 1997/WB Music, 1997.
Best-selling record by Aqua from the album *Aquarium* (MCA, 97).

Long Neck Bottle
Words and music by Steve Wariner and Rick Carnes.
Steve Wariner, 1997/PSO Ltd., 1997/Songs of Peer, 1997.
Best-selling record by Garth Brooks from the album *Sevens* (Capitol Nashville, 97).

The Look of Love
Words and music by Burt Bacharach and Hal David.
Colgems-EMI Music, 1965.
Revived by Susannah Hoffs in the film and on the soundtrack album *Austin Powers* (Hollywood, 97). Also revived by Sean Lennon and Yuka Honda on the album *Great Jewish Music: Burt Bacharach* (Tzadik, 97).

Look into My Eyes
Words and music by Bone and D. J. U-Neek.
Keenu Music, 1997/Mo Thug Music, 1997/Ruthless Attack Muzick, 1997/Dollarz N Sense Musick, 1997.
Best-selling record by Bone Thugs-N-Harmony in the film and on the soundtrack album *Batman and Robin* (Warner Sunset/Warner Brothers, 97).

Looking in the Eyes of Love
Words and music by Kostas Lazarides and Patricia Ann Walker.
Polygram International Music, 1990/Songs of Polygram/Rebel Heart Music.
Revived by Alison Kraus & Union Station on the album *So Long So Wrong* (Rounder, 97). This was previously a hit by Patty Loveless.

Love
Words and music by Charles Strauss and Martin Charnin.
MPL Communications Inc., 1991.
Revived by Terri White on the album *Incurably Romantic* (Original Cast, 97). This is from the 1991 musical *Annie Warbucks*.

Love Gets Me Every Time
Words and music by Shania Twain and Robert John "Mutt" Lange.
Polygram Music Publishing Inc., 1997/Loon Echo Music, 1997/Zomba Music, 1997.
Best-selling record by Shania Twain from the album *Come on Over* (Mercury, 97).

Love Is All We Need
Words and music by James Harris, III, Terry Lewis, Rick James, and Mary J. Blige.
Flyte Tyme Tunes, 1997/EMI-April Music, 1997/Stone City Music, 1997/National League Music, 1997.
Introduced by Mary J. Blige on the album *Share My World* (MCA, 97).

Love Is the Right Place
Words and music by Marcus Hummon and Tommy Sims.
EMI-Christian Music, 1997/Floyd's Dream Music, 1997/Careers-BMG
    Music, 1997/Bases Loaded Music, 1997/MCA Music, 1997.
Best-selling record by Bryan White from the album *The Right Place*
    (Asylum, 97).

Love Minus Zero/No Limit
Words and music by Bob Dylan.
M. Witmark & Sons, 1965.
Revived by Rod Stewart on the album *Diana, Princess of Wales,
    Tribute* (Columbia, 97).

Love and the Weather
Words and music by Irving Berlin
Irving Berlin Music Corp., 1947.
Revived by Susannah McCorkle on the album *Let's Face the Music--
    The Songs of Irving Berlin* (Concord, 97). Introduced by Kate Smith.

Loved Too Much
Words and music by Don Schlitz and Billy Livsey.
New Don Music, 1997/New Haven Music, 1997/Irving Music Inc.,
    1997.
Best-selling record by Ty Herndon on the album *Living In a Moment*
    (Epic, 97).

M

Mack the Knife
Words and music by Kurt Weill, Berthold Brecht, and Marc Blitzstein.
Harms, Inc., 1928.
Revived by Nick Cave on the album *September Songs--The Music of Kurt Weill* (Sony Classics, 97).

Mad About You
Words and music by Paul Reiser and Donald Fagenson.
EMI-Worldtrax Music, 1993/EMI-Intertrax Music, 1993.
Revived by Andrew Gold and Anita Baker on the album *Music from and Inspired by the TV Series Mad About You--The Final Frontier* (Atlantic, 97). Co-writer Fagenson is also known as Don Was. Andrew Gold does the vocal over the credits on the TV show.

A Man This Lonely
Words and music by Ronnie Dunn and Tommy Lee James.
Sony ATV Tree Publishing, 1997/Showbilly, 1997/Still Working for the Man Music, 1997.
Best-selling record by Brooks & Dunn from the album *Brook & Dunn--The Greatest Hits Collection* (Arista, 97).

Marching to Mars
Words and music by Sammy Hagar and Mickey Hart.
WB Music, 1997/The Nine Music, 1997/Spent Bullets Music, 1997/360 Publishers Corp., 1997.
Best-selling record by Sammy Hagar from the album *Marching to Mars* (MCA, 97).

Marilyn
Words and music by Dan Bern.
Kababa Music, Los Angeles, 1997.
Introduced by Dan Bern on the album *Dan Bern* (Work, 97). The song ponders whether Marilyn Monroe would still be alive today if she had married Henry Miller instead of Arthur Miller.

Me Too
Words and music by Toby Keith and Chuck Cannon.
Wacissa River Music, Nashville, 1997/Polygram Music Publishing Inc.,
   1997/Tokeco Music, 1997/So Bizzy Music, 1997.
Best-selling record by Toby Keith from the album *Dream Walkin'*
   (Mercury Nashville, 97).

Medium Rare
Words and music by Kevin Bacon.
Introduced by Damon Fletcher in the movie *Telling Lies in America*.
   This penetrating film is about the early days of rock and roll radio.

Memo from Turner (English)
Words and music by Mick Jagger and Keith Richards.
ABKCO Music Inc., 1970.
Revived by Dramarama on the album *Shared Vision--The Songs of The
   Rolling Stones* (Mercury, 97). This revives one of Jagger's scariest
   vocals, from the movie *Performance*.

The Memory Remains
Words and music by James Hetfield and Lars Ulrich.
Creeping Death Music, 1997.
Best-selling record by Metallica from the album *Reload* (Elektra, 97).

Men in Black
Words and music by Will Smith, Patrice Rushen, Terry McFadden, and
   Fred Washington.
New Columbia Pictures Music, 1997/Baby Fingers Music, 1997/Treyball
   Music, 1997/Tamina Music, 1997/Freddie Dee Music, 1997.
Introduced by Will Smith in the film and on the sountrack album *Men
   in Black* (Columbia, 97). This samples "Forget Me Nots" by Patrice
   Rushen.

Miss Misery
Words and music by Elliot Smith.
Careers-BMG Music, 1997/Spent Bullets Music, 1997.
Introduced by Elliot Smith in the film and on the soundtrack album
   Good Will Hunting (Capitol, 97). The underground singer/songwriter
   made a breakthrough with five songs in the movie. Nominated for an
   Academy Award, Best Song of the Year, 1997.

MmmmBop
Words and music by Isaac Hanson, Taylor Hanson, and Zac Hanson.
Jam N' Bread Music, 1997/Heavy Harmony Music, 1997.
Best-selling record by Hanson from the album *Middle of Nowhere*
   (Mercury, 97). Nominated for a Grammy Award, Best Record of the
   Year, 1997.

Mo Money Mo Problems
Words and music by Christopher Wallace, Steve Jordan, Mason Betha, Bernard Edwards, and Nile Rodgers.
Big Poppa Music, 1997/Justin Combs Music, 1997/EMI-April Music, 1997/Steven A. Jordan Music, 1997/Bernard's Other Music, 1997/ Sony ATV Music, 1997/Mason Betha Music, 1997/Tommy Jymi, Inc., 1997.
Best-selling record by The Notorious B.I.G. (featuring Puff Daddy and Mase) from the album *Life After Death* (Arista, 97).

Monkey Wrench
Words and music by Dave Grohl, George Rutherberg, and Nate Mendel.
MJ12 Music, 1997.
Best-selling record by Foo Fighters from the album *The Colour and the Shape* (Capitol, 97).

The Moon of Manakoora
Words and music by Frank Loesser and Alfred Newman.
Frank Music Co., 1937.
Reissued on Dorothy Lamour's album *The Moon of Manakoora* (ASV, 97). It was first introduced in the film *The Hurricane*.

More Than This (English)
Words and music by Bryan Ferry.
Virgin Songs, 1975.
Revived by 10,000 Maniacs on the album *Love Among the Ruins* (Geffen, 97). This was a classic Roxy Music track.

Mouth (English)
Words and music by Gavin Rossdale.
Mad Dog Winston Music, 1997/Warner-Tamerlane Music, 1997/Truly Soothing Elevator Music, 1997.
Introduced by Bush in the film and on the soundtrack album *An American Werewolf in Paris* (Trauma/ Interscope/ Hollywood, 97).

Much More
Words and music by Harvey Schmidt and Tom Jones.
Chappell & Co., Inc., 1960.
Revived by Betty Buckley on the album *Much More* (Sterling, 97). It was previously from the musical *The Fantasticks*.

Mute Superstar
Words and music by Robert Pollard.
Needmore Music, Minneapolis, 1997.
Introduced by Guided by Voices on the album *Mag Earwhig!* (Matador, 97).

My Baby Daddy
Words and music by Levert Agee, Baron Agee, Maurice White, and

Albert McKay.
Pepper Drive Music, 1997/Raw Cast Music, 1997/EMI-April Music, 1997/Steel Chest Music Inc., 1997/Heavy Harmony Music, 1997.
Best-selling record by B-Rock & the Bizz from the album *And Then There Was Bass* (Laface/Arista, 97).

My Body
Words and music by Darrell Allamby, Lincoln Brouder, and Antoinette Roberson.
2000 Watts Music, Newark, 1997/Toni Robi Music, 1997.
Best-selling record by LSG from the album *Levert-Sweat-Gill* (East West, 97).

My Heart Will Go On (Theme from *Titanic*) (English)
Words and music by James Horner and Will Jennings.
Famous Music Corp., 1997/Ensign Music, 1997/Will Jennings Music, 1997.
Introduced by Celine Dion on the album *The Reason* (Epic, 97) and featured in the film and on the soundtrack album *Titanic*. (Sony Music Soundtrack, 97). Won an Academy Award for Best Song of the Year 1997.

My Love Is the Shhh!
Words and music by James Baker, Melvin Lee Wilson, Jeff Young, Tamara Powell, Sauce, and Rochad Holiday.
Unichappell Music Inc., 1997/Junkie Funk Music, 1997/Tam-Cat Music, 1997.
Best-selling record by Somethin' for the People featuring Trina and Tamara from the album *This Time It's Personal* (Warner Brothers, 97).

My Own Prison
Words and music by Scott Stapp and Mark Tremonti.
Stapp/Tremonti Music, New York, 1997.
Best-selling record by Creed from the album *My Own Prison* (Wind Up, 97).

N

Never Make a Promise
Words and music by Darryl Simmons.
Warner-Tamerlane Music, 1997/Boobie-Loo, 1997.
Best-selling record by Dru Hill from the album *Dru Hill* (Island, 97).

The New Pollution
Words and music by Beck Hanson, Michael Simpson, and John King.
Dust Brothers Music, Los Angeles, 1996/Cyanide Breathmint Music,
 1996/BMG Songs Inc., 1996.
Best-selling record by Beck from the album *Odelay* (DGC, 96).

1969
Words and music by Iggy Pop (pseudonym for James Osterberg).
James Osterberg Music, 1968.
Revived by Joey Ramone on the album *We Will Fall--The Iggy Pop
 Tribute* (Royalty, 97).

No Diggity
Words and music by Teddy Riley, Chauncey Hannibal, Lynise Walters,
 Williams Stewart, and Dr. Dre (pseudonym for Andre Young).
Donril Music, 1996/Zomba Music, 1996/Chauncey Black Music, 1996/
 Smokin' Sounds, 1996/Queen Pen Music, 1996/Sidi Music, 1996/
 Sony ATV Tunes, 1996/Ain't Nothin' Goin on But Music, 1996.
Best-selling record by Blackstreet from the album *Another Level*
 (Blackstreet/Interscope, 96). Won a Grammy Award for Best R&B
 Song 1997.

No Expectations (English)
Words and music by Mick Jagger and Keith Richards.
ABKCO Music Inc., 1968.
Revived by Deana Carter on the album *Stone Country* (Beyond, 97).

No No No
Words and music by Vincent Herbert and Rob Fusari.
Three Boys from Newark Music, 1997/Promiscuous Music, 1997/

Warner-Tamerlane Music, 1997/Sang Melee Music, 1997/Ms. Mary's Music, 1997/Milkman Music, 1997.
Best-selling record by Destiny's Child from the album *Destiny's Child* (Columbia, 97).

Norwegian Wood (English)
Words and music by John Lennon and Paul McCartney.
Sony ATV Songs, 1965/Maclen Music, 1965.
Revived by Cornershop on the album *When I Was Born for the 7th Time* (Luaka Bop/Warner Brothers, 97).

Not an Addict (Belgian)
English words and music by Gert Bettens and Sarah Bettens.
Double T Music (Belgium), 1997.
Best-selling record by K's Choice from the album *Paradise in Me* (550 Music, 97).

Not Tonight
Words and music by Kim Jones, Missy Elliott, Lisa Lopes, Da Brat (pseudonym for Shawntae Harris), Angie Martinez, Ronald Bell, Robert Bell, George Brown, Angie Muhammed, Claydes Smith, James Taylor, Dennis Thomas, and Earl Toon.
Second Decade Music, 1997/Warner-Tamerlane Music, 1997/WB Music, 1997.
Introduced by Lil' Kim, Angie Martinez, Left Eye, Da Brat, and Missy Elliott in the film and on the soundtrack album *Nothing to Lose* (Big Beat, 97).

Nothin' but the Cavi Hit
Words and music by Dedric Rolison, Delmar Arnaud, and Ricardo Brown.
Real an Ruff Music, 1997/Suge Music, 1997/Emoni's Music, 1997/High Priest Music, 1997/Ensign Music, 1997.
Best-selling record by Mack 10 and Tha Dogg Pound in the film and on the soundtrack album *Rhyme and Reason* (Priority, 97).

Nowhere Road
Words and music by Steve Earle and Reno King.
Goldline Music Inc., 1987/WB Music, 1987.
Revived by Willie & Waylon on the album *Wanted! The Outlaws* (RCA, 96). It was a previously unreleased version of the Steve Earle classic.

O

The Oldest Profession
Words and music by Ira Gasman and Cy Coleman.
Notable Music Co., Inc., 1997/Irving Music Inc., 1997.
Introduced by Lillias White in the musical and on the cast album *The Life* (RCA, 97).

On My Own (English)
Words and music by Pascal Gabriel, Paul Statham, and Lisa Lamb.
Warner-Chappell Music, 1997/WB Music, 1997.
Best-selling record by Peach Union from the album *I Peach Union*(Epic, 97).

On & On
Words and music by Erykah Badu and Jaborne Jamal.
Divine Pimp Music, 1997/Tribes of Kedar Music, 1997/BMG Music, 1997/McNooter Music, 1997.
Best-selling record by Erykah Badu from the album *Baduizm* (Universal, 97). Nominated for a Grammy Award, Best R&B Song of the Year, 1997.

On the Verge
Words and music by Hugh Prestwood.
Careers-BMG Music, 1995/Hugh Prestwood, 1995.
Best-selling record by Collin Raye from the album *I Think About You* (Epic, 95).

One Headlight
Words and music by Jakob Dylan.
Brother Jumbo Music, 1996.
Best-selling record by the Wallflowers from the album *Bringing Down the Horse* (Interscope, 96). Won a Grammy Award for Best Rock Song of the Year 1997.

One Hell of a Life
Words and music by Katell Keineg.

Warner-Tamerlane Music, 1997.
Introduced by Katell Keineg on the album *Jet* (Elektra, 97).

The One I Gave My Heart To
Words and music by Diane Warren.
Realsongs, 1996.
Best-selling record by Brandy from the album *One in a Million*
  (Blackground/Atlantic, 96).

One More Hour
Words and music by Corin Tucker and Carrie Brownstein.
Code Word Nemesis, Olympia, 1997.
Introduced by Sleater-Kinney on the album *Dig Me Out* (Kill Rock
  Stars, 97). By far the year's spiciest girl-group.

One More Time (German)
English words and music by Olaf Jeglitza, Jai Wind, and Bret Argovitz.
Copyright Control, 1997.
Best-selling record by Real McCoy from the album *One More Time*
  (Arista, 97).

One Night at a Time
Words and music by Earl Bud Lee, Eddie Kilgallon, and Roger Cook.
EMI-Blackwood Music Inc., 1997/Golly Rogers Music, 1997/Song
  Island Music, 1997/Life's a Pitch Music, 1997/Neon Sky Music,
  1997/Hipp Row Music, 1997.
Best-selling record by George Strait from the album *Carrying Your Love
  with Me* (MCA, 97).

One Song Glory
Words and music by Jonathan Larson.
Finster & Lucy Music, 1996/EMI-April Music, 1996.
Revived by Norbert Leo Butz in the musical *Rent*. This great overlooked
  song in the show jump-started the career of an understudy.

Operator
Words and music by Jim Croce.
MCA Music, 1971/Blendingwell Music, 1971.
Revived by Crystal Bernard on the album *Jim Croce--A Nashville
  Tribute* (River North, 97).

Overnight Sensation
Words and music by Eric Carmen.
Elbo Music, 1974/Eric Carmen Music, 1974/Songs of Polygram, 1974/
  Mondial Lazer Edizioni (Italy), 1974.
Revived by Hushdrops on the album *Raspberries Preserved (a Tribute)*
  (Ginger, 96).

P

Paint It Black (English)
Words and music by Mick Jagger and Keith Richards.
ABKCO Music Inc., 1966.
Revived by Glenn Tipton on the album *Baptizm of Fire* (Atlantic, 97).

Paradise Found (The Uzbeckestan Song)
Words and music by Stan Freeman.
Introduced by Stan Freeman in the musical revue *Secrets Every Smart
   Traveler Should Know*.

Paranoid Android (English)
Words and music by Colin Greenwood, Johnny Greenwood, Ed
   O'Brien, Phil Selway, and Thom Yorke.
Warner-Chappell Music, 1997.
Introduced by Radiohead on the album *OK Computer* (Capitol, 97).

Peach Pickin' Time Down in Georgia
Words and music by Jimmie Rodgers and C. McMichen.
Peer International Corp., 1933.
Revived by Willie Nelson on the album *The Songs of Jimmie
   Rodgers--A Tribute* (Egyptian/Columbia, 97).

Peel Me a Grape
Words and music by David Frishberg.
Saunders Publications, Inc., 1962.
Revived by Diana Krall on the album *Love Scenes* (Impulse, 97).

People Get Ready
Words and music by Curtis Mayfield.
Warner-Tamerlane Music, 1964.
Revived by Ziggy Marley & the Melody Makers on the album *Fallen Is
   Babylon* (Elektra, 97).

Perfect Drug
Words and music by Nine Inch Nails.
TVT, NYC, 1997/Leaving Hope Music, 1997.

Best-selling record by Nine Inch Nails in the film and on the soundtrack album *Lost Highway* (TVT, 96). This was the underground soundtrack of the year.

Pink
Words and music by Glen Ballard, Richard Supa, and Steven Tyler.
Swag Song Music, 1997/Aerostation Corp., 1997/MCA Music, 1997/ Super Supa Songs, 1997.
Best-selling record by Aerosmith from the album *Nine Lives* (Columbia, 97).

Places I've Never Been
Words and music by Tony Martin, Reese Wilson, and Aimee Mayo.
Hamstein Cumberland, Nashville, 1997/Baby Mae Music, Austin, 1997/ New Haven Music, 1997.
Best-selling record by Mark Wills from the album *Mark Willis* (Mercury Nashville, 97).

Please
Words and music by Troy Haseldon.
We've Got the Music, Nashville, 1997/Ashwords Music, Chicago, 1997/ Polygram Music Publishing Inc., 1997.
Best-selling record by the Kinleys from the album *Just Between You and Me* (Epic, 97).

Please Don't Go (German)
English words and music by Franz Reuter, Peter Bischof-Fallenstein, Marty Cintron, and Mary Applegate.
Far M. V., 1996/BMG Music, 1996.
Best-selling record by No Mercy from the album *No Mercy* (Arista, 96).

Precious Declaration
Words and music by Ed Roland.
Sugarbuzz Music, 1997.
Best-selling record by Collective Soul from the album *Disciplined Breakdown* (Atlantic, 97).

Pretty Little Adriana
Words and music by Vince Gill.
Benefit Music, 1996.
Best-selling record by Vince Gill from the album *High Lonesome Sound* (MCA, 96).

Push
Words and music by Matt Serletic and Rob Thomas.
Melusic Music, 1997/EMI-Blackwood Music Inc., 1997/Bidnis Inc Music, 1997.
Best-selling record by Matchbox 20 from the album *Yourself or Someone Like You* (Atlantic, 97).

Put Your Hands Where My Eyes Could See
Words and music by Trevor Smith, Darrol Durant, R. Munroe, and
  Jimmy Seals.
AlshaMighty, 1997/T'Ziah's Music, 1997/Acuff Rose Music.
Best-selling record by Busta Rhymes from the album *When Disaster
  Strikes* (Elektra, 97).

Q

Quit Playing Games (with My Heart) (Swedish-German)
English words and music by Max Martin and Herbert Crichlow
Zomba Music, 1997/Creative Science Music, 1997/Megasongs, 1997.
Best-selling record by Backstreet Boys from the album *Backstreet Boys*
(Jive, 97).

R

The Rain (Supa Dupa Fly)
Words and music by Missy Elliot, Tim Mosley, Donald Bryant, Ann
  Peebles, and Kenneth Miller.
WB Music, 1997/Irving Music Inc., 1997.
Best-selling record by Missy Elliott from the album *Supa Dupa Fly*
  (East West, 97).

Rambler '65
Words and music by Ben Vaughan.
Mob Control, Brooklyn, 1996.
Introduced by Ben Vaughan on the album *Rambler '65* (Rhino, 96).
  This was a tribute to one of the favorite cars of the Baby Boom
  generation. Vaughan was responsible for the music behind *Third Rock
  from the Sun*.

Real Wild Child
Words and music by John O'Keefe, John Greenan, and David Owens.
Wren Music Co., Inc., 1957.
Revived by Joan Jett on the album *We Will Fall--The Iggy Pop Tribute*
  (Royalty, 97). It was previously recorded by Jerry Lee Lewis, and
  Ivan, a.k.a. Jerry Allison of the Crickets.

Red Bluff
Words and music by Mike Watt.
tHUNDERSPIEL, 1997/Bug Music, 1997.
Introduced by Mike Watt on the album *Contemplating the Engine Room*
  (Columbia, 97).

Request Line
Words and music by Renee Neufville, K. Gee, Darren Lighty, Nick
  Ashford, and Valerie Simpson.
9th Town Music, 1997/Naughty, 1997/Yah Yah Music, 1997/Do What I
  Gotta Music, 1997/Nick-O-Val Music, 1997.
Best-selling record by Zhane from the album *Saturday Night* (Motown,
  97).

The Rest of Mine
Words and music by Trace Adkins and Jan Beard.
WB Music, 1997/Sawng Country Music, 1997/Milene Music, 1997/
   Loggy Bayou Music, 1997.
Best-selling record by Trace Adkins from the album *Big Time* (Capitol
   Nashville, 97).

Return of the Mack
Words and music by Mark Morrison.
SPZ, 1997.
Best-selling record by Mark Morrison from the album *Return of the
   Mack* (Atlantic, 97).

Rikety Tikety Tin
Words and music by Tom Lehrer.
Maelstrom Music, Cambridge, 1967.
Revived by Barbara Manning on the album *1212* (Matator, 97).

Rumble in the Jungle
Words and music by Lauryn Hill, Wyclef Jean, Benny Andersson, Stig
   Anderson, Prakazrel Michel, Bjorn Ulvaeus, John Forte, Trevor
   Smith, Malik Taylor, Chip Taylor, and John Davis.
Sony ATV Music, 1997/Zomba Music, 1997/EMI-Blackwood Music
   Inc., 1997/EMI-Grove Park Music, 1997/Warner-Tamerlane Music,
   1997.
Introduced by Fugees, A Tribe Called Quest, Busta Rhymes and Forte
   in the film and on the soundtrack album *When We Were Kings* (DAS/
   Mercury, 97). The movie was about an epic Ali-Foreman fight.

Rumor Has It
Words and music by Clay Walker and M. Jason Greene.
Lori Jayne Music, Nashville, 1997/Sondaddy Music, Nashville, 1997/
   Muy Bueno Music, 1997.
Best-selling record by Clay Walker from the album *Rumor Has It*
   (Reprise, 97).

Running Out of Reasons to Run
Words and music by George Teren and Bob Regan.
Zomba Music, 1997/AMR, 1997/Sierra Home, 1997.
Best-selling record by Rick Trevino from the album *Learning as You
   Go* (Columbia, 97).

S

Sad Lookin' Moon
Words and music by Randy Owen, Teddy Gentry, and Greg Fowler.
Maypop Music, 1997.
Best-selling record by Alabama from the album *Dancin' on the Boulevard* (RCA, 97).

The Saint
Words and music by Edwin Astley.
EMI-Miller Catalogue, 1967.
Revived by Orbital in the film and on the soundtrack album *The Saint* (Virgin, 97).

Santeria
Words and music by Sublime.
MCA Music, 1997/Gasoline Alley Music/Lou Dog Music, 1997.
Best-selling record by Sublime from the album *Sublime* (MCA, 97).

Say You'll Be There (English)
Words and music by Melanie Brown, Geraldine Halliwell, Victoria Adams, Melanie Chisholm, Emma Lee Burton, and Elliot Kennedy.
Full Keel Music, 1997/Windswept Pacific, 1997/Sony ATV Songs, 1997.
Best-selling record by the Spice Girls from the album *Spice* (Virgin, 97).

Say...If You Feel Alright
Words and music by James Harris, III, Terry Lewis, Crystal Waters, Maurice White, Albert McKay, and Allee Willis.
EMI-April Music, 1997/Flyte Tyme Tunes, 1997/Crystal Waters Music, 1997/Famous Music Corp., 1997/Steel Chest Music Inc., 1997/EMI-Blackwood Music Inc., 1997/Irving Music Inc., 1997.
Best-selling record by Crystal Waters from the album *Crystal Waters* (Mercury, 97).

Secret Garden
Words and music by Bruce Springsteen.
Bruce Springsteen Publishing, 1995.
Revived by Bruce Springsteen in the film and on the soundtrack album *Jerry McGuire* (Epic Soundtrax, 96). Best-selling record by Bruce Springsteen.

Semi-Charmed Life
Words and music by Stephan Jenkins.
3EB Music, 1997.
Best-selling record by Third Eye Blind from the album *Third Eye Blind* (Elektra, 97).

Send Back My Heart
Words and music by George Ducas and John David.
Polygram International Music, 1997.
Best-selling record by Gary Alban from the album *Used Heart for Sale* (Decca, 96).

September Song (American-German)
English words and music by Kurt Weill and Maxwell Anderson.
DeSylva, Brown & Henderson, Inc., 1938/Hampshire House Publishing Corp., 1938.
Revived by Betty Carter on the album *I'm Yours, You're Mine* (Verve, 97). Also revived by Lou Reed on the album *September Songs--The Music of Kurt Weill* (Sony Classics, 97).

Serenity
Words and music by Susan Birkenhead and Jeffrey Stock.
Chappell & Co., Inc., 1997.
Introduced by Betty Buckley in the musical *Triumph of Love* (97).

Sex and Candy
Words and music by John Wozniak.
John Wozniak Music, Floral Park, 1997.
Best-selling record by Marcy Playground from the album *Marcy Playground* (Mammoth/Capitol, 97).

The Shake
Words and music by Jim McElroy and Butch Carr.
Log Rhythm Music, 1997/Millhouse Music, 1997.
Best-selling record by Neal McCoy from the album *Be Good at It* (Atlantic, 97).

Shame on Us
Words and music by Jonatha Brooke.
Dog Dream, 1997.
Introduced by Jonatha Brooke on the album *10 Cent Wings* (MCA, 97).

Shame on You
Words and music by Amy Ray.
Virgin Music, 1997/Godhap Music, 1997.
Introduced by Indigo Girls on the album *Shaming of the Sun* (Epic, 97).

She Ain't Goin' Nowhere
Words and music by Guy Clark.
Chappell & Co., Inc., 1976.
Revived by Nanci Griffith on the album *Blue Roses from the Moon*
(Elektra, 97).

She Drew a Broken Heart
Words and music by Jim McElroy and Ned McElroy.
Log Rhythm Music, 1997.
Best-selling record by Patty Loveless from the album *The Trouble with
the Truth* (Epic, 96).

She Said, He Heard
Words and music by Suzy Bogguss and Don Schlitz.
Loyal Duchess Music, 1997/Famous Music Corp., 1997/New Agency
Music, 1997/New Hayes Music, 1997/Don Schlitz Music.
Introduced by Suzy Bogguss on the album *Give Me Some Wheels*
(Capitol, 97).

She's Got It All
Words and music by Drew Womack and Craig Wiseman.
Emdar Music, 1997/Texas Wedge Music, 1997/Womaculate Conception
Music, 1997/Almo Music Corp., 1997/Daddy Rabbitt Music, 1997.
Best-selling record by Kenny Chesney from the album *I Will Stand*
(BNA, 97).

She's Sure Taking It Well
Words and music by Tim Buppert, Don Pfrimmer, and George Teren.
Miss Betsy Music, 1996/Tiny Buckets O'Music, 1996/G.I.D. Music,
1996/Zomba Music, 1996.
Best-selling record by Kevin Sharp from the album *Measure of a Man*
(Asylum, 96).

She's Taken a Shine
Words and music by Greg Garnhill and Richard Bach.
Emdar Music, 1996, 1996/Bayou Liberty Music, 1996/Full Keel Music,
1996/Texas Wedge Music, 1996.
Best-selling record by John Berry from the album *Faces* (Capitol
Nashville, 96).

Show Me Love (Swedish)
English words and music by Robyn Carlsson and Max Martin.
Heavy Rotation Music, 1997/Cheiron Music, 1997/BMG Music, 1997.
Best-selling record by Robyn from the album *Robyn Is Here* (RCA, 97).

Shy
Words and music by Ani DiFranco.
Righteous Babe Music, Buffalo, 1995.
Revived by Ani DiFranco on the album *Living in Clip* (Righteous Babe, 97). This feminist force field broke through with a live album.

Sign of the Times
Words and music by Chris DeGarmo.
Ryche Trax Music, San Francisco, 1997.
Best-selling record by Queensryche from the album *Hear in the Now Frontier* (EMI, 97).

Silver Springs
Words and music by Stevie Nicks.
Barbara Nicks Music, 1977/Wixen Music, 1997.
Revived by Fleetwood Mac featuring Stevie Nicks on the live album *The Dance* (Reprise, 97). It was initially the B-side of "Go Your Own Way."

Sister Morphine (English)
Words and music by Mick Jagger, Keith Richards, and Marianne Faithfull.
ABKCO Music Inc., 1971.
Revived by Marianne Faithfull on the album *Shared Vision--The Songs of The Rolling Stones* (Mercury, 97).

Sittin' on Go
Words and music by Josh Leo and Rick Bowles.
Warner-Tamerlane Music, 1996/Hellmaymen, 1996/Maypop Music, 1996/Nineteenth Hole Music, 1996/Mike Curb Productions, 1996/Diamond Storm Music, 1996.
Best-selling record by Bryan White from the album *Between Now and Forever* (Asylum, 97).

Six Days on the Road
Words and music by Earl Green and Carl Montgomery.
Tree Publishing Co., Inc., 1963/Southern Arts Music, 1963.
Revived by Sawyer Brown on the album *Six Days on the Road* (Curb, 97). This was a Dave Dudley classic.

6 Underground (English)
Words and music by Chris Corner, Ian Pickering, and Liam Howlett.
BMG Music, 1997/EMI Music Publishing, 1997.
Best-selling record by Sneaker Pimps from the film and on the soundtrack album *The Saint* (Virgin, 97). Also on the album *Becoming X* (Clean up/Virgin, 97).

Slow Ride
Words and music by Mark Selby, Danny Tate, and Kenny Wayne

Shepherd.

Music Corp. of America, 1997/Bro N' Sis Music, 1997/Only Hit Music, 1997.

Revived by Kenny Wayne Shepherd Band on the album *Trouble Is* (Revolution, 97).

Smile

Words and music by Brad Jordan, Mike Dean, and Tupac Shakur.

N-The Water Publishing, 1997/Still N-The Water Music, 1997/Joshua's Dream Music, 1997/Interscope Pearl, 1997/Warner-Tamerlane Music, 1997.

Best-selling record by Scarface featuring 2Pac and Johnny P. from the album *The Untouchable* (Virgin, 97).

Smokin' Me Out

Words and music by Warren Griffin, Ronald Isley, Rudolph Isley, Ernie Isley, Marvin Isley, O'Kelly Isley, and Chris Jasper.

Bovina Music, Inc., 1997/EMI-April Music, 1997/Warren G Music, 1997.

Best-selling record by Warren G. Featuring Ronald Isley from the album *Take a Look over Your Shoulder* (Mercury, 97).

So Help Me Girl

Words and music by Howard Perdew and Andrew Spooner.

Modar Music, 1995/Songwriters Ink, 1995/Longitude Music, 1995/ Emdar Music, 1995/Texas Wedge Music, 1995/Full Keel Music, 1995.

Revived by Gary Barlow on the album *Open Road* (Arista, 97). This was a recent Joe Diffie's hit.

Sock It 2 Me

Words and music by Missy Elliott.

Mass Confusion Music, 1997/Virginia Beach Music, 1997/Michael Shore Music, 1997/Wadud Music, 1997/Warner-Tamerlane Music, 1997/Throwin' Tantrums Music, 1997/Air Control Music, 1997/EMI-April Music, 1997.

Best-selling record by Missy Elliott from the album *Supa Dupa Fly* (East West, 97).

Somedays (English)

Words and music by Paul McCartney.

MPL Communications Inc., 1997.

Introduced by Paul McCartney on the album *Flaming Pie* (Capitol, 97).

Someone

Words and music by Sean "Puffy" Combs, Kit Walker, Graham, Harve Pierre, Kelly Price, Christopher Wallace, Chris Martin, and Todd Shaw.

Justin Combs Music, 1997/EMI-April Music, 1997/Dub's World Music,
   1997/HGL Music, 1997/Harve Pierre Music, 1997/Rhythm Blunt
   Music, 1997/Price is Right Music, 1997/MCA Music, 1997.
Best-selling record by SWV featuring Puff Daddy from the album
   Release Some Tension (RCA, 97).

Something About the Way You Look Tonight (English)
Words and music by Elton John and Bernie Taupin.
Polygram Music Publishing Inc., 1997/William A. Bong Music, 1997.
Best-selling record by Elton John from the album *The Big Picture*
   (Rocket, 97).

Something Bigger Than Me
Words and music by Steve Dorff and Marty Panzer.
Swanee Bravo Music, 1997/Dorffmeister Music, 1997.
Introduced by Dolly Parton in TV special *Annabelle's Wish* (Rising
   Tide, 97).

Something That We Do
Words and music by Skip Ewing and Clint Black.
Acuff Rose Music, 1997/Blackened Music, 1997.
Best-selling record by Clint Black from the album *Nothing but the
   Taillights* (RCA Nashville, 97).

Something's Got Me
Words and music by Lori Carson.
Feels Good for a Minute Music, 1997/Sony ATV Songs, 1997.
Introduced by Lori Carson on the album *Everything I Got Runs Wild*
   (Restless, 97).

A Song for Mama
Words and music by Babyface (pseudonym for Kenny Edmunds).
Sony ATV Songs, 1997/Ecaf Music, 1997/Fox Film Music Corp., 1997.
Best-selling record by Boys II Men in the film and on the soundtrack
   album *Soul Food* (Laface/Arista, 97).

Song2 (English)
Words and music by Damon Albarn, Graham Coxon, Steven James, and
   David Rowntree.
EMI-Blackwood Music Inc., 1997.
Best-selling record by Blur from the album *Blur* (Virgin, 97).

Space Jam
Words and music by Johnny McGowan, Nathan Orange, and Albert
   Bryant.
Quadrasound Music, 1996/Warner-Chappell Music, 1996.
Best-selling record by Quad City DJ's in the film and on the soundtrack
   album *Space Jam* (Warner Sunset/Atlantic, 96).

Spell
Words and music by Allen Ginsberg and Oliver Ray.
May King Poetry Music, 1997/Yam Gruel Music, 1997.
Introduced by Patti Smith on the album *Peace and Noise* (Arista, 97).
  This song featured Allen Ginsberg's poem "Footnote to Howl."

Spice Up Your Life (English)
Words and music by Richard Stannard, Matt Rowe, Melanie Brown,
  Geraldine Halliwell, Victoria Adams, Melanie Chisholm, and Emma
  Lee Burton.
Full Keel Music, 1997/Windswept Pacific, 1997/Polygram International
  Music, 1997.
Best-selling record by the Spice Girls from the album *Spice* (Virgin,
  97).

Springtime for Hitler
Words and music by Mel Brooks.
Legation Music, New York, 1967.
Revived by Mel Brooks, Dick Shawn and Chorus on the soundtrack
  album *The Producers* (Razor & Tie/BMG, 97).

Stairway to Heaven (English)
Words and music by Jimmy Page and Robert Plant.
Superhype Publishing, 1972.
Revived by Pat Boone on the album *In a Metal Mood* (Hip-O, 97).

Staring at the Sun (Irish)
Words and music by U2, Bono (pseudonym for Paul Hewson), and The
  Edge (pseudonym for Dave Evans).
Polygram Music Publishing Inc., 1997.
Best-selling record by U2 from the album *Pop* (Island, 97).

Step by Step (English)
Words and music by Annie Lennox.
Lennoxa Music, 1997/BMG Music, 1997.
Best-selling record by Whitney Houston in the film and on the
  soundtrack album *The Preacher's Wife* (Arista, 97).

Step into a World (Rapture's Delight)
Words and music by Jess Williams, Chris Stein, Debbie Harry,
  Lawrence Parker, and Harry Palmer.
Embassy Music Corp., 1997/Zomba Music, 1997/Chrysalis Music
  Group, 1997/Largo Music, Inc., 1997.
Best-selling record by KRS-One from the album *I Got Next* (Jive, 97).

Still
Words and music by Maury Yeston.
Yeston Music, Ltd., 1997.

Introduced by Larry Keith and Alma Cuervo in the musical and on the cast album *Titanic* (RCA Victor, 97).

Still Holding On
Words and music by Clint Black, Matraca Berg, and Marty Stuart.
Longitude Music, 1997/Wedgewood Avenue Music, 1997/Blackened Music, 1997/Great Broad Music, 1997/Marty Party Music, 1997.
Best-selling record by Clint Black and Martina McBride from the album *Evolution* (RCA Nashville, 97).

Stomp
Words and music by George Clinton, Jr., Kirk Franklin, Walter Morrison, and Gary Shider.
Bridgeport Music Inc., 1997/Lilly Mack, 1997.
Best-selling record by God's Property featuring Kirk Franklin and "Salt" from the album *God's Property from Kirk Franklin's Nu Nation* (B-Rite/Interscope, 97). It makes use of "One Nation Under a Groove" by Funkadelic. Nominated for a Grammy Award, Best R&B Song, 1997.

Strawberry Wine (Life Is Sweet)
Words and music by Pat Giraldo and Neil Giraldo.
Bel Chiasso Music, 1997/Spyder Mae, 1997.
Introduced by Pat Benetar on the album *Insomniac* (CMC International, 97).

Summertime (English)
Words and music by David Gavurin and Harriet Wheeler.
David Gavurin (England), 1997/Harriet Wheeler (England), 1997.
Introduced by The Sundays on the album *Static & Silence* (DGC, 97).

Sunny Came Home
Words and music by Shawn Colvin and John Leventhal.
WB Music, 1997/Scred Songs, 1997/Lev-a-Tunes, 1997.
Best-selling record by Shawn Colvin from the album *A Few Small Repairs* (Columbia, 97). Won Grammy Awards.

Surrounded (Canadian)
Words and music by Chantal Kreviazuk.
Sony ATV Music, 1997/Neverwouldahot Music, 1997.
Introduced by Chantal Kreviazuk on the album *Under These Rocks and Stones* (Columbia, 97).

The Sweetest Sounds
Words and music by Richard Rodgers.
Williamson Music, 1962.
Revived by Brandy and Paolo Montalban in the TV special *Rodgers & Hammerstein's Cinderella*. This was added to the TV special from the musical *No Strings*.

Sweetheart on the Barricades (English)
Words and music by Richard Thompson.
Polygram Music Publishing Inc., 1997.
Introduced by Richard Thompson and Danny Thompson on the album
  Industry (Hannibal, 97).

T

Take It to the Streets
Words and music by Roger McNair, Billy Lawrence, Rashad Smith, A. Colon, G. Underwood, and B. Reed.
Ramp Music, 1997/B. K. L. Music, 1997/WB Music, 1997/Sadiyah Music, 1997/Armacien Music, 1997/Brown Lace, 1997/Keep On, 1997/Unidisc Music, 1997.
Best-selling record by Rampage featuring Billy Lawrence from the album *Scout's Honor By Way of Blood* (Elektra, 97).

Taneytown
Words and music by Steve Earle.
WB Music, 1997/South Nashville Music, 1997.
Introduced by Steve Earle on the album *El Corazon* (Warner Brothers, 97).

Telephone Road
Words and music by Steve Earle.
WB Music, 1997/South Nashville Music, 1997.
Introduced by Steve Earle on the album *El Corazon* (Warner Brothers, 97).

Tell Him (American-Canadian)
Words and music by David Foster, Linda Thompson, and Walter Afanasieff.
Warner-Tamerlane Music, 1997/One For Three, 1997/Brandon & Brody Music, 1997/Peer Music, 1997/Wally Songs, 1997/Sony ATV Music, 1997.
Introduced by Celine Dion and Barbra Streisand on the album *The Reason* (Epic, 97). It was also on Streisand's album *Higher Ground* (Columbia, 97).

Thank God for Believers
Words and music by Mark Alan Springer, Roger Springer, and Tim Johnson.
EMI-Blackwood Music Inc., 1997/Mark Alan Springer Music, 1997/Big

Giant Music, 1997.
Best-selling record by Mark Chesnutt from the album *Thank God for Believers* (Decca, 97).

That's What I Hear in These Sounds
Words and music by Dar Williams.
Burning Field Music, 1997/Bug Music, 1997.
Introduced by Dar Williams on the album *End of the Summer* (Razor & Tie, 97).

That's When I Reach for My Revolver (English)
Words and music by Clint Conley.
Lambent Music, Concord, 1981.
Revived by Mission of Burma on the album *Signals, Calls & Marches* (Rykodisc, 97). It was also revived by Animal Rights on the album *Moby* (Elecktra, 97).

Theme from *The Valley of the Dolls*
Words and music by Andre Previn and Dory Previn.
Twentieth Century-Fox Music Corp., 1972.
Revived by k.d. lang on the album *Drag* (Warner Brothers, 97). The song was previously introduced by Dionne Warwick.

There Goes
Words and music by Alan Jackson.
Yee Haw Music, Nashville, 1996/WB Music.
Best-selling record by Alan Jackson from the album *Everything I Love* (Arista, 96).

They Like It Slow
Words and music by Shazaam Connor, John Connor, and Darryl Jackson.
John Doe Music, Hendersonville, 1997/Baby Boy Music, 1997/G. I. Music, 1997.
Best-selling record by H-Town from the album *Ladies Edition* (Relativity, 97).

They Live in You (He Lives in You)
Words and music by Mark Mancina, Lebo M., and Jay Rifkin.
Wonderland Music, 1997.
Introduced by Samuel E. Wright in the musical and on the cast album *The Lion King* (Walt Disney, 97). It is easily the best of several songs added to the Broadway production.

Things'll Never Change
Words and music by Earl Stevens, Mike Mosley, and Bruce Hornsby.
WB Music, 1996/Zappo Music, 1996/Zomba Music, 1996/E-Forty Music, 1996/Steady Mobbin', 1996/EMI-Blackwood Music Inc., 1996.

Best-selling record by E-40 Featuring Bo-Rock from the album *Tha Hall of Game* (Jive, 96).

Thinking of You
Words and music by Rafael Saadiq, Dwayne Wiggins, and Timothy Riley.
Polygram International Music, 1997/Tony! Toni! Tone!, 1997.
Best-selling record by Tony!Toni!Tone! from the album *House of Music* (Mercury, 96).

Thirty-Three
Words and music by Billy Corgan.
Chrysalis Music Group, 1995/Cinderful Music, 1995.
Best-selling record by Smashing Pumpkins from the album *Mellon Collie and the Infinite Sadness* (Virgin, 95).

(This Ain't) No Thinkin' Thing
Words and music by Tim Nichols and Mark D. Sanders.
EMI-Blackwood Music Inc., 1996/Tyland Music, 1996/Starstruck Writers Group, 1996/Mark D. Music, 1996.
Best-selling record by Trace Adkins from the album *Dreamin' Out Loud* (Capitol Nashville, 96).

This Is the Moment (American-English)
Words and music by Leslie Bricusse and Frank Wildhorn.
Cherry River Music Co., 1995/Stage-Screen Music, Inc., 1995.
Introduced by Robert Cuccioli in the musical and on the cast album *Jekyll & Hyde* (Atlantic Theater, 97).

This Night Won't Last Forever
Words and music by Bill LaBounty and Ron Freeland.
Careers-BMG Music, 1976.
Revived by Sawyer Brown on the album *Six Days on the Road* (Curb, 97).

This Woman's Work (English)
Words and music by Kate Bush.
Kate Bush Music, Ltd., London, England, 1988/Screen Gems-EMI Music Inc., 1988.
Revived by Maxwell on the album *MTV Unplugged* (Columbia, 97).
The classic Kate Bush weeper from the climactic scene of the movie *She's Having a Baby*.

Three Marlenas
Words and music by Jakob Dylan.
Brother Jumbo Music, 1996.
Best-selling record by the Wallflowers from the album *Bringing Down the Horse* (Interscope, 96).

3AM
Words and music by Matt Serletic and Rob Thomas.
Melusic Music, 1997/EMI-Blackwood Music Inc., 1997/Bidnis Inc Music, 1997.
Best-selling record by Matchbox 20 from the album *Yourself or Someone Like You* (Lava/Atlantic, 97).

The Tide Is High (Jamaican)
Words and music by John Holt.
Gemrod Music, Inc., 1968.
Revived by Jazz Passengers featuring Deborah Harry on the album *Individually Twisted* (32 Records, 97). The reggae favorite was a hit for Harry's old band, Blondie.

Titanic
Words and music by Keith Gattis and Kostas Lazarides.
Hornbill Music, 1997/Songs of Polygram, 1997/Seven Angels Music, 1997.
Introduced by Keith Gattis in the film and on the soundtrack album *Switchback* (RCA, 97).

To Make You Feel My Love
Words and music by Bob Dylan.
Special Rider Music, 1997.
Best-selling record by Billy Joel from the album *Billy Joel--Greatest Hits, Volume 3* (Columbia, 97). Introduced by Bob Dylan on the album *Time out of Mind* (Columbia, 97).

To the Moon and Back (Australian)
Words and music by Darren Hayes and Damon Jones.
Rough Cut Music, 1997/EMI-Blackwood Music Inc., 1997.
Best-selling record by Savage Garden from the album *Savage Garden* (Columbia, 97).

Today My World Slipped Away
Words and music by Mark Wright and Vern Gosden.
Polygram Music Publishing Inc., 1980/Hook 'N B, 1980/Polygram International Music, 1980.
Best-selling record by George Strait from the album *Carrying Your Love with Me* (MCA Nashville, 97).

Together Again
Words and music by James Harris, III, Terry Lewis, Janet Jackson, and Rene Elizondo.
Black Ice Music, 1997/EMI-April Music, 1997/Flyte Tyme Tunes, 1997.
Best-selling record by Janet Jackson from the album *Velvet Rope* (Virgin, 97).

Tomorrow Never Dies
Words and music by Sheryl Crow and Mitchell Froom.
Old Crow, Los Angeles, 1997/Warner-Tamerlane Music, 1997/United
Lion Music Inc., 1997.
Introduced by Sheryl Crow in the film and on the soundtrack album
Tomorrow Never Dies (A & M, 97).

Tonight
Words and music by Stephen Sondheim and Leonard Bernstein.
Chappell & Co., Inc., 1957.
Revived by Porno for Pyros on the album *Mom II--Music for Our
Mother Ocean* (Surfdog/Interscope, 97).

Tonight's the Night (Gonna Be Alright)
Words and music by Rod Stewart.
EMI-April Music, 1976.
Revived by by Janet Jackson on the album *Velvet Rope* (Virgin, 97).

Too Gone Too Long
Words and music by Diane Warren.
Realsongs, 1997.
Best-selling record by En Vogue from the album *EV3* (Atlantic, 97).

Touch, Peel and Stand
Words and music by Travis Meeks.
Scrogrow Music, 1997.
Best-selling record by Days of the New from the album *Days of the
New* (Geffen, 97).

Tourniquet
Words and music by Marilyn Manson (pseudonym for Brian Warner).
Beat up Your Mom Music, 1997/Dinger & Ollie Music, 1997/Onward
(England), 1997.
Introduced by Marilyn Manson on the album *Antichrist Superstar*
(Nothing Intersco pe, 97).

Trailways Bus
Words and music by Paul Simon and Derek Walcott.
Paul Simon Music, 1997.
Introduced by Paul Simon on the album *Songs from the Capeman*
(Warner Brothers, 97). Introduced by Ruben Blades and Philip
Hernandez in the musical *The Capeman*.

Trenchtown Rock (Jamaican)
Words and music by Bob Marley.
Polygram International Music, 1971.
Revived by Sublime on the album *Second Hand Smoke* (Gasoline Alley/
MCA, 97). Nouveau-reggae band updates the master.

Triumph
Words and music by Wu-Tang Clan.
Wu-Tang Music, 1997/Careers-BMG Music, 1997.
Introduced by Wu-Tang Clan on the album *Wu-Tang Forever* (RCA, 97).

The Trouble with the Truth
Words and music by Gary Nicholson.
Sony ATV Music, 1996.
Best-selling record by Patty Loveless from the album *The Trouble with the Truth* (Epic, 96).

Truly Madly Deeply (Australian)
Words and music by Darren Hayes and Damon Jones.
Rough Cut Music, 1997/EMI-Blackwood Music Inc., 1997.
Best-selling record by Savage Garden from the album *Savage Garden* (Columbia, 97).

Trust
Words and music by Dave Mustaine and Marty Friedman.
Mustaine Music, 1997/Screen Gems-EMI Music Inc., 1997/Adam Martin Music.
Best-selling record by Megadeth from the album *Cryptic Writings* (Capitol, 97).

Trying to Get to Heaven
Words and music by Bob Dylan.
Special Rider Music, 1997.
Introduced by Bob Dylan on the album *Time out of Mind* (Columbia, 97). It is an emotional centerpiece of his first studio album in years.

Tubthumping (English)
Words and music by Chumbawamba.
Cherry Music, 1997/Leo Song (England).
Best-selling record by Chumbawamba from the album *Tubthumper* (Republic/Universal, 97).

Turn My Head
Words and music by Live.
Loco De Amor, New York, 1997/Behind Bars, 1997.
Best-selling record by Live from the album *Secret Samadhi* (MCA, 97).

2 Become 1 (English)
Words and music by Melanie Brown, Geraldine Halliwell, Victoria Adams, Melanie Chisholm, Emma Lee Burton, Richard Stannard, and Matt Rowe.
Full Keel Music, 1997/Windswept Pacific, 1997/Polygram International Music, 1997.

Best-selling record by the Spice Girls from the album *Spice* (Virgin, 97).

Two Sleepy People
Words and music by Frank Loesser and Hoagy Carmichael.
Famous Music Corp., 1938.
Revived by Carly Simon and John Travolta on the album *Film Noir* (Arista, 97). John Travolta is everywhere this year, even back on record.

U

Unchained Melody
Words and music by Alex North and Hy Zaret.
Frank Music Co., 1955.
Best-selling record by LeAnn Rimes from the album *Unchained Melody/ The Early Years* (Curb, 97).

The Unforgiven
Words and music by James Hetfield and Lars Ulrich.
Creeping Death Music, 1994.
Revived by Apocalyptica on the album *Apocalyptica Plays Metallica by Four Cellos* (Mercury, 97). This was this year's most unusual mismatch.

Unhook the Stars
Words and music by Cyndi Lauper and Janet Pulsford.
Rella Music Corp., 1997.
Introduced by Cyndi Lauper in the film *Unhook the Stars*. It is also on the album *Sisters of Avalon* (Epic, 97).

Up Jumps Da Boogie
Words and music by Tim Mosley, Melvin Barcliff, and Missy Elliott.
Virginia Beach Music, 1997/Magoo Music, 1997/Mass Confusion Music, 1997.
Best-selling record by Timbaland and Magoo from the album *Welcome to Our World* (Atlantic, 97).

87

V

Valentine
Words and music by Jack Kugell and Jim Brickman.
EMI-April Music, 1997.
Best-selling record by Jim Brickman with Martina McBride from the
album *Picture This* (Windham Hill, 97).

Van Halen
Words and music by Nerf Herder.
WB Music, 1997.
Introduced by Nerf Herder on the album *Nerf Herder* (Arista, 97). This
is rock criticism at its finest.

Velvet Waltz
Words and music by Doug Martsch.
All Smiles Music, 1997.
Introduced by Built to Spill on the album *Perfect from Now On* (Warner
Brothers, 97).

Virtual Insanity (English)
Words and music by Jay Kay and Toby Smith.
EMI-Blackwood Music Inc., 1997.
Best-selling record by Jamiroquai from the album *Travelling Without
Moving* (Work, 97).

Volcano Girls
Words and music by Nina Gordon.
Are You There God It's Me, Chicago, 1997.
Best-selling record by Veruca Salt from the album *Eight Arms to Hold
You* (Geffen, 97).

W

Walkin' on the Sun
Words and music by Robert Delevante.
Who's Your Daddy Music, 1997/Warner-Tamerlane Music, 1997.
Best-selling record by Smash Mouth from the album *Fush Yu Mang* (Interscope, 97).

Wannabe (English)
Words and music by Melanie Brown, Geraldine Halliwell, Victoria Adams, Melanie Chisholm, Emma Lee Burton, Richard Stannard, and Matt Rowe.
Full Keel Music, 1997/Windswept Pacific, 1997/Polygram International Music, 1997.
Best-selling record by the Spice Girls from the album *Spice* (Virgin, 97). This group ignited a "Beatlemania" the Bangles only could have wish for.

Watch Me Do My Thing
Words and music by Chris Stokes, Claudio Cueni, and Kel.
Zomba Music, 1997/Hookman Music, 1997/Fe-Mac Music, 1997.
Best-selling record by Immature featuring Smooth and Ed from Good Burger in the film and on the soundtrack album *All That Matters* (RCA, 97).

Watch This
Words and music by Anthony Smith, Aaron Barker, and Ron Harpin.
Notewrite Music, 1997/Words to Music, 1997/O-Tex Music, 1997/Blind Sparrow Music, 1997/Sony ATV Cross Keys Publishing Co. Inc., 1997/Kim Williams, 1997.
Best-selling record by Clay Walker from the album *Rumor Has It* (Giant/Warner Brothers, 97).

We Danced Anyway
Words and music by Matraca Berg and Randy Scruggs.
Longitude Music, 1996/August Wind Music, 1996/Great Broad Music, 1996/Heart of Hearts Music, 1996.

Best-selling record by Deana Carter from the album *Did I Shave My Legs for This* (Capitol Nashville, 96).

We Have Explosive (English)
Words and music by Future Sound of London.
Sony ATV Music, 1997.
Introduced by Future Sound of London on the album *Dead Cities* (Astralwerks, 97).

We Live on Borrowed Time
Words and music by David Friedman.
Midder Music, New York, 1993.
Introduced by Nancy Lamott on the album *What's Good About Goodbye* (Midder Music, 97). This posthumous anthem for the cabaret culture was also performed by Jason Alexander.

We Trying to Stay Alive (English)
Words and music by Barry Gibb, Robin Gibb, Maurice Gibb, Wyclef Jean, Prakazrel Michel, and John Forte.
Gibb Brothers Music, 1977.
Revived by Wyclef Jean featuring Refugee Allstars on the album *Carnival* (Ruffhouse/Columbia, 97). It is a take-off of the Bee Gees' "Stayin' Alive."

We Were in Love
Words and music by Chuck Cannon and Allen Shamblin.
Wacissa River Music, Nashville, 1996/CMI America, 1996/Built on Rock Music, 1996/Song Matters Music, 1996/Famous Music Corp., 1996.
Best-selling record by Toby Keith from the album *Dream Walkin'* (Mercury, 96).

We're Not Making Love No More
Words and music by Babyface (pseudonym for Kenny Edmunds).
Sony ATV Songs, 1997/Ecaf Music, 1997/Fox Film Music Corp., 1997.
Introduced by Dru Hill in the film and on the soundtrack album *Soul Food* (Laface/Arista, 97).

What About Us
Words and music by Tim Mosley and Missy Elliott.
Virginia Beach Music, 1997/Mass Confusion Music, 1997/Warner-Chappell Music, 1997.
Best-selling record by Total in the film and on the soundtrack album *Soul Food* (Laface/Arista, 97).

What Good Can Drinking Do
Words and music by Janis Joplin.
Strong Arm Music, 1962.
Revived by Tracy Nelson on the album *Blues Down Deep: Songs of*

Janis Joplin (House of Blues, 97). This was Joplin's first song, revived by the resurgent belter Nelson.

What the Heart Wants
Words and music by Michael Dulaney.
Moon Catcher Music, 1997/Son of a Gila Monster Music, 1997.
Best-selling record by Collin Raye from the album *The Best of Collin Raye: Direct Hits* (Epic, 97).

What If
Words and music by Nick Ashford, Valerie Simpson, and Maya Angelou.
Nick-O-Val Music, 1997/Guycol Music, 1997.
Introduced by Ashford & Simpson with Maya Angelou on the album *Been Found* (Hopsack and Silk, 97).

What They Do
Words and music by Tarik Collins, Tahmir Thompson, Leonard Hubbard, Jimmy Grey, and Rafael Saadiq.
Careers-BMG Music, 1997/Grand Negaz Music, 1997/Godfather Music, 1997.
Best-selling record by the Roots from the album *Illadelph Half Life* (Geffen, 97).

What a Way to Live
Words and music by Steve Krikorian.
Polygram International Music, 1990.
Revived by Tonio K. on the album *Ole (The Persistence of Memory)* (Gadfly, 97).

What the World Needs Now
Words and music by Burt Bacharach and Hal David.
New Hidden Valley Music Co., 1965/Casa David, 1965.
Revived by Burt Bacharach in the film and on the soundtrack album *Austin Powers* (Hollywood, 97). Burt sings this on screen in the movie, which also features prominent product placement of one of his obscure solo LPs.

Whatever
Words and music by Babyface (pseudonym for Kenny Edmunds), Guiliano Franco, and Keith Andes.
Sony ATV Songs, 1997/Ecaf Music, 1997/No Intro Music, 1997/E2 Music, 1997/EMI-April Music, 1997/Kejanda Music, 1997.
Best-selling record by En Vogue from the album *EV3* (Elektra, 97).

Whatever Comes First
Words and music by Walt Aldridge, Brad Crisler, and Drew Womack.
Emdar Music, 1997/Texas Wedge Music, 1997/Rick Hall Music, 1997/Womaculate Music, 1997.

Best-selling record by Sons of the Desert from the album *Whatever Comes First* (Epic, 97).

What's on Tonight
Words and music by Montell Jordan, Devante, and James Earl Jones.
Chrysalis Music Group, 1996/Mo Swang Music, 1996/EMI-April Music, 1996/Baji, 1996/Deswing Mob, 1996.
Best-selling record by Montell Jordan from the album *More* (Mercury, 96).

Wheat Penny
Words and music by Greg Kendall.
Sky Songs, 1997/Polygram Music Publishing Inc., 1997.
Introduced by The Circus Monkeys in the film and on the soundtrack album *Bandwagon* (Milan, 97).

Wheels of a Dream
Words and music by Lynn Ahrens and Stephen Flaherty.
Warner-Chappell Music, 1997.
Introduced by Audra McDonald and Brian Stokes Mitchell in the musical and on the cast album *Ragtime* (RCA, 97).

When I Close My Eyes
Words and music by Mark Alan Springer and Nettie Musick.
Tom Collins Music Corp., 1997/Murrah, 1997.
Best-selling record by Kenny Chesney from the album *I Will Stand* (BNA, 97).

When You Care
Words and music by Steve Schalchlin.
Introduced by the cast in the musical and on the cast album *The Last Session* (High Time/Bonus Round, 97).

Whenever, Wherever, Whatever
Words and music by Maxwell Menard and Stuart Matthewman.
Sony ATV Tunes, 1997.
Revived by by Maxwell on the album *MTV Unplugged* (Columbia, 97).

Where Corn Don't Grow
Words and music by Roger Murrah and Mark Alan Springer.
Tom Collins Music Corp., 1996/Murrah, 1996.
Best-selling record by Travis Tritt from the album *The Restless Kind* (Warner Brothers, 96).

Where Have All the Cowboys Gone
Words and music by Paula Cole.
Hingface Music, 1997/Ensign Music, 1997.
Best-selling record by Paula Cole from the album *This Fire* (Warner

Brothers, 97). Nominated for Grammy Awards, Best Record of the Year, 1997 and Best Song of the Year, 1997.

While You're Waiting (English)
Words and music by Ron Sexsmith.
Interscope Pearl, 1997/Warner-Tamerlane Music, 1997/Ron Boy Rhymes Music, 1997.
Introduced by Ron Sexsmith on the album *Other Songs* (Interscope, 97).

Who Used to Dance
Words and music by Abbey Lincoln.
Moseka Music, 1997.
Introduced by Abbey Lincoln on the album *Who Used to Dance* (Verve, 97).

Who Will Love Me as I Am
Words and music by Bill Russell and Henry Kreiger.
Introduced by Alice Ripley and Emily Skinner in the musical *Side Show*.

Who's Cheatin' Who
Words and music by Jerry Hayes.
Songs of Polygram, 1980/EMI-Algee Music, 1980.
Best-selling record by Alan Jackson from the album *Everything I Love* (Arista, 96).

Why Would I Say Goodbye
Words and music by Kix Brooks and Chris Waters.
Buffalo Prairie Songs, 1997/Chris Waters Music, 1997/Sony ATV Tree Publishing, 1997.
Best-selling record by Brooks & Dunn from the album *Brooks & Dunn- -The Greatest Hits Collection* (Arista, 97).

Wichita Lineman
Words and music by Jim Webb.
Polygram International Music, 1968.
Revived by Dwight Yoakam on the album *Under the Covers* (Warner Brothers, 97).

The Winner
Words and music by Artis Ivey, Jr., Brian Dobbs, and Curtis Mayfield.
Boo Daddy Music, 1996/T-Boy Music Publishing Co., Inc., 1996/Wino Funk Music, 1996/Warner-Tamerlane Music, 1996.
Introduced by Coolio and L.V. in the film and on the soundtrack album *Space Jam* (Warner Sunset/Atlantic, 96).

Wishin' and Hopin'
Words and music by Burt Bacharach and Hal David.
New Hidden Valley Music Co., 1963/Casa David, 1963.

Revived by Ani DiFranco in the film and on the soundtrack album *My Best Friend's Wedding* (Work/Sony Music Soundtrack, 97).

The World Tonight (English)
Words and music by Paul McCartney.
MPL Communications Inc., 1997.
Introduced by Paul McCartney in the film *Father's Day* and on the album *Flaming Pie* (Capitol, 97).

Y

You Are Not My First Love
Words and music by Bart Howard and Pete Windsor.
Walden Music, Inc., 1953.
Revived by KT Sullivan on the album *In Other Words: The Songs of Bart Howard* (DRG, 97). This was introduced by Mabel Mercer.

You Bring Me Up
Words and music by K-Ci Hailey, JoJo Hailey, and Big Yam.
Mike's Rap Music, Valencia, 1997/EMI-April Music, 1997/LBN Music, 1997/Cord Kayla Music, 1997.
Best-selling record by K-Ci & JoJo from the album *Love Always* (MCA, 97).

You Can Leave Your Hat On
Words and music by Randy Newman.
Randy Newman Music, 1972.
Revived by Tom Jones in the film and on the soundtrack album *The Full Monty* (RCA Victor, 97). It was the best usage of a song since Joe Cocker's rendition in the movie *9-1/2 Weeks*.

You Don't Have to Hurt No More
Words and music by Keirston Lewis, Jeffrey Allen, Ricky Kinchen, Stanley Williams, Lawrence Waddell, and Howie O'Dell.
Mint Factory Music, 1997/EMI-April Music, 1997.
Best-selling record by Mint Condition from the album *Definition of a Band* (A & M, 96).

You Light Up My Life
Words and music by Joe Brooks.
Polygram Music Publishing Inc., 1977/Curb Songs, 1997.
Revived by LeAnn Rimes on the album *You Light Up My Life* (Curb, 97).

You Make Me Wanna...
Words and music by Jermaine Dupri, Manuel Seal, and Usher Raymond.

EMI-April Music, 1997/So So Def Music, 1997/Slack A. D. Music, 1997/UR IV Music, 1997.
Best-selling record by Usher from the album *My Way* (Laface/Arista, 97).

You Should Be Mine (Don't Waste Your Time)
Words and music by Sean "Puffy" Combs, Ronald Lawrence, Mason Betha, Kelly Price, James Brown, Steve Jordan, and Brian McKnight.
EMI-April Music, 1997/O/B/O/Itself, 1997/Justin Combs Music, 1997/ Ausar Music, 1997/Mason Betha Music, 1997/MCA Music, 1997/ Price is Right Music, 1997/Dynatone Music, 1997.
Best-selling record by Brian McKnight featuring Mase from the album *Anytime* (Mercury, 97).

You Were Meant for Me
Words and music by Jewel Kilcher.
Wiggly Tooth Music, 1996/Polio Boy Music, 1996/Third Story Music Inc., 1996/WB Music, 1996.
Best-selling record by Jewel from the album *Pieces of You* (Atlantic, 96).

You and You Alone
Words and music by Vince Gill.
Benefit Music, 1996.
Best-selling record by Vince Gill from the album *High Lonesome Sound* (MCA Nashville, 96).

Your Woman (English)
Words and music by Jyoti Mishra.
Copyright Control, 1997.
Best-selling record by White Town from the album *Women in Technology* (EMI, 97).

You're the Inspiration (American-Canadian)
Words and music by Peter Cetera and David Foster.
BMG Songs Inc., 1978/Foster Frees Music Inc., 1997/Warner-Tamerlane Music, 1997.
Revived by Peter Cetera on the album *Peter Cetera--Greatest Hits* (River North, 97).

Lyricists & Composers Index

Lyricists & Composers Index

Lyricists & Composers Index

Lyricists & Composers Index

108

King, Reno
  Nowhere Road
Kipner, Steve
  Invisible Man
Kirkland, Scott
  Busy Child
Kolanek, Gregory
  Counting Blue Cars
Kool & the Gang
  Feel So Good
Krakower, Kevin
  Dream
Krawinkel, Gert
  Da Da Da I Don't Love You You
    Don't Love Me
Kreiger, Henry
  Who Will Love Me as I Am
Kreviazuk, Chantal
  Surrounded
Krikorian, Steve
  What a Way to Live
Kugell, Jack
  Valentine
Kulick, Bruce
  Jungle
LaBounty, Bill
  This Night Won't Last Forever
Lamb, Lisa
  On My Own
lang, k.d.
  Anybody Seen My Baby
Langan, Greg
  Firestarter
Lange, Robert John "Mutt"
  I'll Always Be Right There
  Love Gets Me Every Time
Larkin, Patty
  Brazil
Larkins, R.
  Honey
Larson, Jonathan
  One Song Glory
Lauper, Cyndi
  Unhook the Stars
Lawrence, Billy
  Take It to the Streets
Lawrence, Ronald
  Hypnotize

You Should Be Mine (Don't Waste
  Your Time)
Lawrence, Tracy
  How a Cowgirl Says Goodbye
Lawson, Billy
  I Left Something Turned on at Home
Lazarides, Kostas
  Looking in the Eyes of Love
  Titanic
LeBlanc, Lenny
  Falling
Lee, Earl Bud
  One Night at a Time
Lehrer, Tom
  Rikety Tikety Tin
Leitch, Donovan
  Legend of a Cowgirl
Lennon, John
  Norwegian Wood
Lennox, Annie
  Step by Step
Leo, Josh
  Sittin' on Go
Lerum, Kenny
  For You
Leslie, Steve
  Let It Rain
Leventhal, John
  Sunny Came Home
Lewis, Keirston
  You Don't Have to Hurt No More
Lewis, Terry
  Everything
  4 Seasons of Loneliness
  Got Till It's Gone
  If We Fall in Love Tonight
  Love Is All We Need
  Say...If You Feel Alright
  Together Again
Lighty, Darren
  Butta Love
  Request Line
Lincoln, Abbey
  Who Used to Dance
Linzer, Sandy
  I Believe in You and Me
Live
  Freaks

113

Smith, Elliot
  Angeles
  Miss Misery
Smith, Pete
  I Shot the Sheriff
Smith, Rashad
  Take It to the Streets
Smith, Stephony
  Go Away
  How Was I to Know
  It's Your Love
Smith, Toby
  Virtual Insanity
Smith, Trevor
  Put Your Hands Where My Eyes
    Could See
  Rumble in the Jungle
Smith, Will
  Men in Black
Sobule, Jill
  Bitter
Sondheim, Stephen
  Tonight
Soulshock
  I Love Me Some Him
South, Joe
  Hush
Spooner, Andrew
  So Help Me Girl
Springer, Mark Alan
  Thank God for Believers
  When I Close My Eyes
  Where Corn Don't Grow
Springer, Roger
  It's a Little Too Late
  Let It Rain
  Thank God for Believers
Springfield, Rick
  Jessie's Girl
Springsteen, Bruce
  4th of July, Asbury Park (Sandy)
  It's Hard to Be a Saint in the City
  Secret Garden
Stacy, Ralph
  In My Bed
Stamos, Mark
  Find My Way Back to My Heart

Stanley, Paul
  Jungle
Stannard, Richard
  Spice Up Your Life
  2 Become 1
  Wannabe
Stapp, Scott
  My Own Prison
Statham, Paul
  On My Own
Steele, Jeffrey
  If You Love Somebody
Stefani, Eric
  Don't Speak
Stefani, Gwen
  Don't Speak
Stefl, Charlie
  The Fool
Stein, Chris
  Step into a World (Rapture's Delight)
Stephenson, Karl
  Dream
Stevens, Earl
  Things'll Never Change
Stevens, Jeff
  Carrying Your Love with Me
Stewart, Gloria
  I Love Me Some Him
Stewart, Rod
  Tonight's the Night (Gonna Be
    Alright)
Stewart, Williams
  No Diggity
Sting
  I'll Be Missing You
  I'm So Happy I Can't Stop Crying
Stock, Jeffrey
  Serenity
Stokes, Chris
  Watch Me Do My Thing
Straughter, Henry
  C U When U Get There
Straughter, Maleek
  C U When U Get There
Strauss, Charles
  Love
Struzick, Edward
  Falling

Lyricists & Composers Index

Important Performances Index

Songs are listed under the works in which they were introduced or given significant renditions. The index is organized into major sections by performance medium: Album, Movie, Musical, Performer, Revue, Television Show.

123

I Can Love You
Love Is All We Need
Shared Vision--The Songs of The Rolling
    Stones
    Memo from Turner
    Sister Morphine
Sheryl Crow
    A Change
    Everyday Is a Winding Road
Side Show
    Who Will Love Me as I Am
Signals, Calls & Marches
    That's When I Reach for My Revolver
Sisters of Avalon
    Unhook the Stars
Six Days on the Road
    Six Days on the Road
    This Night Won't Last Forever
Slip Stitch and Pass
    Cities
So Long So Wrong
    Find My Way Back to My Heart
    Looking in the Eyes of Love
So Much for the Afterglow
    Everything to Everyone
Somewhere More Familiar
    All for You
Songbook (A Collection of Hits)
    In Another's Eyes
Songs from a Parent to a Child
    Daydream
Songs from the Capeman
    Bernadette
    I Was Born in Puerto Rico
    Trailways Bus
The Songs of Jimmie Rodgers--A Tribute
    In the Jailhouse Now
    Peach Pickin' Time Down in Georgia
Soul Food
    I Care 'Bout You
    A Song for Mama
    We're Not Making Love No More
    What About Us
South Saturn Delta
    Drifter's Escape
Space Jam
    For You I Will
    I Believe I Can Fly

I Turn to You
    Space Jam
    The Winner
Spice
    Say You'll Be There
    Spice Up Your Life
    2 Become 1
    Wannabe
Static & Silence
    Summertime
Still Climbing
    5 Miles to Empty
Still Waters
    Alone
Stone Country
    No Expectations
Straight on Till Morning
    Carolina Blues
Strangest Places
    Four Leaf Clover
Sublime
    Santeria
Sunday Morning to Saturday Night
    Back When We Were Beautiful
Supa Dupa Fly
    The Rain (Supa Dupa Fly)
    Sock It 2 Me
Surfacing
    Building a Mystery
Switchback
    Titanic
Take a Look over Your Shoulder
    I Shot the Sheriff
    Smokin' Me Out
Ten Cent Wings
    Shame on Us
10,000 Angels
    A Girl's Gotta Do What a Girl's Gotta
    Do
Tha Hall of Game
    Things'll Never Change
Thank God for Believers
    Thank God for Believers
Third Eye Blind
    How's It Gonna Be
    Semi-Charmed Life

Movie

Important Performances Index

137

Revue

Television Show

Awards Index

A list of songs nominated for Academy Awards by the Academy of Motion Picture Arts and Sciences and Grammy Awards from the National Academy of Recording Arts and Sciences. Asterisks indicate the winners; multiple listings indicate multiple nominations.

1997

Academy Award
  Go the Distance
  How Do I Live
  Journey to the Past
  Miss Misery
  My Heart Will Go On (Theme from
    Titanic)*
Grammy Award
  All the Good Ones Are Gone
  Bitch
  Butterfly Kisses*
  Crash into Me
  Criminal
  Did I Shave My Legs for This

The Difference
Don't Speak
Everyday Is a Winding Road
Honey
How Do I Live
I Believe I Can Fly
In Another's Eyes
It's Your Love
MmmmBop
No Diggity*
On & On
One Headlight*
Stomp
Sunny Came Home*
Where Have All the Cowboys Gone

List of Publishers

A directory of publishers of the songs included in *Popular Music,* 1997. Publishers that are members of the American Society of Composers, Authors, and Publishers or whose catalogs are available under ASCAP license are indicated by the designation (ASCAP). Publishers that have granted performing rights to Broadcast Music, Inc., are designated by the notation (BMI). Publishers whose catalogs are represented by The Society of Composers, Authors and Music Publishers of Canada, are indicated by the designation (SOCAN). Publishers whose catalogs are represented by SESAC, Inc., are indicated by the designation (SESAC).

The addresses were gleaned from a variety of sources, including ASCAP, BMI, SOCAN, SESAC, and *Billboard* magazine. As in any volatile industry, many of the addresses may become outdated quickly. In the interim between the book's completion and its subsequent publication, some publishers may have been consolidated into others or changed hands. This is a fact of life long endured by the music business and its constituents. The data collected here, and throughout the book, are as accurate as such circumstances allow.

A

ABKCO Music Inc. (BMI)
1700 Broadway
New York, New York 10019

Above the Rim Music (ASCAP)
see BMG Music

Abra Songs (ASCAP)
see Warner-Chappell Music

Acuff Rose Music (BMI)
65 Music Square West
Nashville, Tennessee 37203

Aerostation Corp. (ASCAP)
16214 Morrison St.
Encino, California 91436

AGF Music Ltd. (ASCAP)
30 W. 21st St.
7th Fl.
New York, New York 10010

Ain't Nothin' Goin on But Music (ASCAP)
see Sony ATV Music

Air Control Music (ASCAP)
see EMI Music Publishing

List of Publishers

Alabama Band Music Co. (ASCAP)
PO Box 121192
Nashville, Tennessee 37212

J. Albert & Sons Music (ASCAP)
c/o Freddy Bienstock Ent.
1619 Broadway, 11th Fl.
New York, New York 10019

All Around Town Music (BMI)
see Sony ATV Music

All Smiles Music (ASCAP)
see BMG Music

Alley Music (BMI)
1619 Broadway, 11th Fl.
New York, New York 10019

Almo/Irving
1358 N. LaBrea
Los Angeles, California 90028

Almo/Irving Music (BMI)
1358 N La Brea
Los Angeles, California 90028

Almo Music Corp. (BMI)
360 N. La Cienega
Los Angeles, California 90048

AlshaMighty
Address Unavailable

Am Music (ASCAP)
see EMI Music Publishing

Amani Music (ASCAP)
see Warner-Chappell Music

American Momentum (BMI)
c/o Mizmo Enterprises
2106 W. Magnolia Blvd.
Burbank, California 91506

American Romance Music (ASCAP)
c/o CMI America
1102 17th Ave. S., Ste. 401
Nashville, Tennessee 37212

AMR (ASCAP)
54 Music Sq. E.
Nashville, Tennessee 37203

Are You There God It's Me (ASCAP)
1330 M State St., No. 128
Chicago, Illinois 60610

Armacien Music (BMI)
see Warner-Chappell Music

Artbyme Music (BMI)
see EMI Music Publishing

Arzo Music (ASCAP)
110 W. 57th St., 7th Fl.
New York, New York 10019

Ash Belle Music (ASCAP)
see Ensign Music

Ashwords Music (BMI)
PO Box 994
Chicago, Illinois 60693

Asleep in the Boat Music (BMI)
see Buddy Killen Music

Assorted Music (BMI)
Attn: Earl Shelton
309 S. Broad St.
Philadelphia, Pennsylvania 19107

Audible Sun (BMI)
1775 Broadway, 7th Fl.
New York, New York 10019

August Wind Music (BMI)
see Longitude Music

Ausar Music (BMI)
see EMI Music Publishing

B

B. Black Music (ASCAP)
see EMI Music Publishing

B. K. L. Music (BMI)
see Warner-Chappell Music

Baby Boy Music (BMI)
see John Doe Music

Baby Fingers Music (ASCAP)
c/o Gary L. Gilbert Esq.
Blum, Bloom, Dekom, & Hercott
150 S Rodeo Dr.
3rd Fl.
Beverly Hills, California 90212

Baby Mae Music (BMI)
c/o Hamstein
PO Box 163870
Austin, Texas 78716

Badams Music (ASCAP)
see Almo Music Corp.

Badazz Music (ASCAP)
see Almo Music Corp.

Baji (BMI)
see Chrysalis Music Group

Banana Tunes Music (BMI)
see BMG Music

Martin Bandier Music
see Entertainment Co. Music Group

Richard Barone Music (BMI)
see Warner-Chappell Music

Base Pipe Music (ASCAP)
see Warner-Chappell Music

Bases Loaded Music (ASCAP)
see Polygram Music Publishing Inc.

Bayou Bay Music (BMI)
see Reynsong Music

Bayou Liberty Music (ASCAP)
see Reynsong Music

BDP Music (ASCAP)
see Zomba Music

Beane Tribe Music (ASCAP)
see EMI Music Publishing

Beat up Your Mom Music (BMI)
see Dinger & Ollie Music

Beechwood Music (BMI)
see EMI Music Publishing

Beef Puppet (ASCAP)
see MCA Music

Behind Bars (ASCAP)
see Warner-Chappell Music

Bel Chiasso Music (ASCAP)
Address Unavailable

Bellboy Music (BMI)
Attn: Earl Shelton
309 S. Broad St.
Philadelphia, Pennsylvania 19107

Benefit Music (BMI)
7250 Beverly Blvd
Los Angeles, California 90036

Irving Berlin Music Corp. (ASCAP)
1290 Avenue of the Americas
New York, New York 10019

Bernard's Other Music (BMI)
see Warner-Chappell Music

Bldnis Inc Music (BMI)
see EMI Music Publishing

Big Fig Music (ASCAP)
see Famous Music Corp.

Big Giant Music (BMI)
see Warner-Chappell Music

Big P Music (BMI)
1651 South Lubdill, No. 102178
Baton Rouge, Louisiana 70806

Big Poppa Music (ASCAP)
see EMI Music Publishing

Big Sky Music (ASCAP)
PO Box 860, Cooper Sta.
New York, New York 10276

Big Tractor Music (ASCAP)
see Warner-Chappell Music

Bigger Than Peanut Butter Music (BMI)
see EMI Music Publishing

Bird Ankles Music
  c/o Chris Williamson
  Olivia Records
  4400 Market St.
  Oakland, California 94608

Black Bull Music (BMI)
  Attn: Stevland Morris
  4616 Magnolia Blvd.
  Burbank, California 91505

Black Ice Music (BMI)
  see Flyte Tyme Tunes

Blackened Music (BMI)
  c/o Prager & Fenton
  12424 Wilshire Blvd., Ste. 1000
  Los Angeles, California 90025

Blendingwell Music (ASCAP)
  94 Grand Ave.
  Englewood, New Jersey 07631

Bleu Disque Music (ASCAP)
  see Warner-Chappell Music

Mary J. Blige (ASCAP)
  see MCA, Inc.

Blind Sparrow Music (BMI)
  see Sony ATV Music

Blue Desert Music (BMI)
  see Windswept Pacific

Blue Horn Toad (BMI)
  see Bug Music

Blue Turtle
  see Magnetic Music Publishing Co.

BMG Music (ASCAP)
  1540 Broadway
  New York, New York 10036

BMG Songs Inc. (ASCAP)
  8370 Wilshire Blvd.
  Beverly Hills, California 90211

Bob-a-Lew Music (ASCAP)
  PO Box 8649
  11622 Valley Spring Ln.
  Universal City, California 91608

Bobby Robinson Music (BMI)
  see Zomba Music

William A. Bong Music
  see Warner-Chappell Music

Boo Daddy Music (ASCAP)
  see T-Boy Music Publishing Co., Inc.

Boobie-Loo (BMI)
  see Warner-Chappell Music

Bovina Music, Inc. (ASCAP)
  c/o Mae Attaway
  330 W. 56th St., Apt. 12F
  New York, New York 10019

Brandon & Brody Music (BMI)
  see Warner-Chappell Music

Bridgeport Music Inc. (BMI)
  c/o Sam Peterer Music
  530 E. 76th St.
  New York, New York 10021

Bring the Noize Music (BMI)
  see Def American Songs

Brio Blues Music (ASCAP)
  see Almo Music Corp.

Bro N' Sis Music (BMI)
  see Keith Sykes Music

Brother Jumbo Music (ASCAP)
  c/o Gelfand Rennert & Feldman
  1880 Century Park E., Ste. 900
  Los Angeles, California 90067

Brown Girl Music (ASCAP)
  see Warner-Chappell Music

Brown Lace (BMI)
  see Zomba Music

Bubalas (SOCAN)
  see BMG Music

Buchu Music (ASCAP)
c/o Haber Corp.
16830 Ventura Blvd.
Encino, California 91436

Buffalo Prairie Songs (BMI)
see Sony ATV Tree Publishing

Bug Music (BMI)
Bug Music Group
6777 Hollywood Blvd., 9th Fl.
Hollywood, California 90028

Bughouse (ASCAP)
c/o Bug Music Group
6777 Hollywood Blvd., 9th Floor
Hollywood, California 90028

Built on Rock Music (ASCAP)
see Ensign Music

Bumstead (SOCAN)
1616 W. 3rd Ave.
Vancouver, British Columbia V6J1K2
Canada

Burning Field Music (BMI)
see Bug Music

Burrin Avenue Music (BMI)
6430 Sunset Blvd., Ste 900
Hollywood, California 90028

C

Caddagh Hill Music (BMI)
see EMI Music Publishing

Careers-BMG Music
see BMG Music

Eric Carmen Music (BMI)
see Polygram Music Publishing Inc.

Casa David (ASCAP)
c/o Hal David
12711 Ventura Blvd., Ste. 420
Studio City, California 91604

Casadida (ASCAP)
see EMI Music Publishing

Castle Bound Music (SESAC)
see Major Bob Music

Castle Street (ASCAP)
1109 16th Ave. S.
Nashville, Tennessee 37212

Catch the Boat Music (ASCAP)
1019 17th Ave. S., Ste. 202
Nashville, Tennessee 37212

Cat's Eye Music (BMI)
see Major Bob Music

Cayman Music (ASCAP)
c/o David Steinberg Esq.p.
Rita Marley Music Div.
North American Bldg., 20th Fl.
121 Broad St.
Philadelphia, Pennsylvania 19107

CBS Songs Ltd. (ASCAP)
see EMI April Canada

Chappell & Co., Inc. (ASCAP)
see Warner-Chappell Music

Chauncey Black Music (ASCAP)
see MCA, Inc.

Check Man Music (ASCAP)
see Warner-Chappell Music

Cheiron Music (ASCAP)
see Zomba Music

Cherry Lane Music Co. (ASCAP)
110 Midland Ave.
Port Chester, New York 10573

Cherry Music (BMI)
see MCA Music

Cherry River Music Co. (BMI)
see Cherry Lane Music Co.

Chrysalis Music Group (ASCAP)
9255 Sunset Blvd., No. 319
Los Angeles, California 90069

Chyna Baby Music (BMI)
see EMI Music Publishing

Cinderful Music (BMI)
  see Chrysalis Music Group

CLR Music (ASCAP)
  see Warner-Chappell Music

CMI America (ASCAP)
  1102 17th Ave. S.
  Nashville, Tennessee 37212

Coburn Music (BMI)
  see Bug Music

Code Word Nemesis (ASCAP)
  120 NE State St., No. 418
  Olympia, Washington 98501

Cody River Music (ASCAP)
  15030 Ventura Blvd., Ste. 3535
  Sherman Oaks, California 91403

Colgems-EMI Music (ASCAP)
  see EMI Music Publishing

Tom Collins Music Corp. (BMI)
  Box 121407
  Nashville, Tennessee 37212

Colour'd Music (ASCAP)
  see PSO Music

Colt-N-Twins Music (BMI)
  see Polygram Music Publishing Inc.

Janice Combs Music (ASCAP)
  see EMI Music Publishing

Justin Combs Music (ASCAP)
  see EMI Music Publishing

Common Green Music (BMI)
  see Rondor Music Inc.

Constant Pressure Music (BMI)
  see Warner-Chappell Music

ControlMusic (BMI)
  see Warner-Chappell Music

Conversation Tee Music (ASCAP)
  see Zomba Music

Copyright Control
  Address Unavailable

Cord Kayla Music (ASCAP)
  see EMI Music Publishing

Ryan Cory Music (BMI)
  2845 38th Ave. S.
  Minneapolis, Minnesota 55406

Country Road Music (ASCAP)
  c/o Gelfand, Rennert & Feldman
  1880 Century Park E.
  Los Angeles, California 90067

Country Road Music Inc. (BMI)
  c/o Gelfand, Rennert & Feldman
  Attn: Babbie Green
  1880 Century Park, E., No. 900
  Los Angeles, California 90067

Crack Music (BMI)
  see Almo/Irving Music

Crazy Cat Catalogue (ASCAP)
  see EMI Music Publishing

Crazy Owl Music (BMI)
  see EMI Music Publishing

Creation Music (BMI)
  see Sony ATV Music

Creative Science Music (ASCAP)
  see Zomba Music

Creeping Death Music (ASCAP)
  c/o Manatt Phelps Rothenberg & Tunn
  ey
  11355 W. Olympic Blvd.
  Los Angeles, California 90064

Crooked Chimney Music (BMI)
  see MCA Music

Crystal Waters Music (ASCAP)
  see Polygram Music Publishing Inc.

Mike Curb Productions (BMI)
  948 Tourmaline Dr.
  Newbury Park, California 91220

Curb Songs
see Mike Curb Productions

Cyanide Breathmint Music (ASCAP)
see BMG Music

D

Daaa!!! Music (ASCAP)
see Human Rhythm

Daddy Rabbitt Music (ASCAP)
see Almo/Irving

Danica Music (BMI)
see Almo/Irving Music

D.A.R.P. Music (ASCAP)
see Diva One

David Z Music (BMI)
11377 W. Olympic Blvd., Ste. 900
Hollywood, California 90064

Dead Solid Perfect Music (BMI)
see Sony ATV Music

Def American Songs (BMI)
16 W. 22nd St.
New York, New York 10010

Delta Kappa Twang Music (ASCAP)
see MCA Music

Demenoid Deluxe Music (ASCAP)
see Warner-Chappell Music

Desmobile Music Inc. (ASCAP)
c/o C. Winston Simone Mgmt.
1790 Broadway, 10th Fl.
New York, New York 10019

Deswing Mob (ASCAP)
see EMI Music Publishing

DeSylva, Brown & Henderson, Inc. (ASCAP)
609 5th Ave.
New York, New York 10017

Devachan Music (BMI)
36 Warwick Rd.
Watertown, Massachusetts 02172

Diadem Music (SESAC)
see Polygram Music Publishing Inc.

Diamond Cuts Music (BMI)
see Walt Disney Music

Diamond Storm Music (BMI)
see EMI Music Publishing

Dinger & Ollie Music (BMI)
see Duke T

Walt Disney Music (ASCAP)
500 S. Buena Vista St.
Burbank, California 91521

Diva One (ASCAP)
Gelfand, Rennert & Feldman
c/o Michael Bivens
1880 Century Park E., Ste. 900
Los Angeles, California 90067

Divine Pimp Music (ASCAP)
see BMG Music

Do What I Gotta Music (ASCAP)
see EMI Music Publishing

Dofat Music (BMI)
see EMI Music Publishing

Dog Dream (ASCAP)
Box 483
Newton Centre, Massachusetts 02159

Dollarz N Sense Musick (BMI)
see Sony ATV Music

Donril Music (ASCAP)
225 W. 129th St.
New York, New York 10027

Dorffmeister Music (BMI)
see Swanee Bravo Music

Double T Music (Belgium)
Address Unavailable

Double Virgo Music (ASCAP)
see MCA, Inc.

Drug Money Music (BMI)
see EMI Music Publishing

Du It All Music (BMI)
  see Boo Daddy Music

Duane Music, Inc. (BMI)
  c/o Garne Thompson
  PO Box 6174
  Albany, California 94706

Dub's World Music (ASCAP)
  see MCA Music

Duke T (BMI)
  11355 W. Olympic Blvd.
  Los Angeles, California 90064

Duncan Sheik Music (BMI)
  see BMG Music

Dust Brothers Music (ASCAP)
  2384 Panorama Terr.
  Los Angeles, California 90039

Dwarf Music Co., Inc. (ASCAP)
  see Big Sky Music

Dyad Music, Ltd. (BMI)
  c/o Mason & Co.
  400 Park Ave.
  New York, New York 10022

Dynatone Music (BMI)
  see Unichappell Music Inc.

E

E-Forty Music (BMI)
  see Zomba Music

Ecaf Music (BMI)
  see Sony ATV Music

Edition (ASCAP)
  see Warner-Chappell Music

Edition Beam Music
  see Warner-Chappell Music

Elbo Music (BMI)
  see Polygram Music Publishing Inc.

Embassy Music Corp. (BMI)
  24 E. 22nd St.
  New York, New York 10010

Emdar Music (ASCAP)
  see Texas Wedge

EMI-Algee Music (BMI)
  see EMI Music Publishing

EMI April Canada
  Address Unavailable

EMI-April Music (ASCAP)
  see EMI Music Publishing

EMI-Blackwood Music Inc. (BMI)
  see EMI Music Publishing

EMI-Christian Music (ASCAP)
  see EMI Music Publishing

EMI-Grove Park Music (BMI)
  see EMI Music Publishing

EMI-Intertrax Music (BMI)
  see EMI Music Publishing

EMI-Josaha Music (ASCAP)
  see EMI Music Publishing

EMI-Miller Catalogue
  see EMI Music Publishing

EMI Music Publishing
  810 7th Ave.
  New York, New York 10019

EMI-Princeton Street Music (ASCAP)
  see EMI Music Publishing

EMI-Worldtrax Music (ASCAP)
  see EMI Music Publishing

Emoni's Music (ASCAP)
  see Ensign Music

Ensign Music (BMI)
  see Famous Music Corp.

Entertaining Music (BMI)
  see Almo/Irving Music

Entertainment Co. Music Group
40 W. 57th St.
New York, New York 10019

E2 Music (ASCAP)
see EMI Music Publishing

Evergleam Music (BMI)
see Rondor Music Inc.

Excellent Classical Songs (BMI)
see Roshashauna

Excellorec Music Co., Inc. (BMI)
1011 Woodland St.
Nashville, Tennessee 37206

F

Fall River Music Inc. (BMI)
250 W. 57th St., Ste. 2017
New York, New York 10019

Famous Music Corp. (ASCAP)
10635 Santa Monica Blvd.
Ste. 300
Los Angeles, California 90025

Far M. V. (SESAC)
see BMG Music

Farrenuff (BMI)
see Windswept Pacific

Fat Hat Music (ASCAP)
see Human Rhythm

The Fat Rat Music (ASCAP)
see EMI Music Publishing

Fe-Mac Music (ASCAP)
see Zomba Music

Feed Them Kids Music (BMI)
see Sony ATV Music

Feels Good for a Minute Music (BMI)
see Sony ATV Music

FHW Music (ASCAP)
8900 Wilshire Blvd., Ste.300
Beverly Hills, California 90211

Finster & Lucy Music (ASCAP)
see EMI Music Publishing

Floyd's Dream Music (ASCAP)
see BMG Music

Flying Rabbi Music (ASCAP)
c/o Jason Finn
915 E. Harrison, Ste. 201
Seattle, Washington 98102

Flyte Tyme Tunes (ASCAP)
c/o Margo Matthews
Box 92004
Los Angeles, California 90009

Foray (SESAC)
see EMI Music Publishing

Foreign Imported (BMI)
8921 S.W. Tenth Terrace
Miami, Florida 33174

Fox Film Music Corp. (BMI)
c/o Twentieth Century Fox Film Corp
PO Box 900
Beverly Hills, California 90213

Frank Music Co. (ASCAP)
see MPL Communications Inc.

Freddie Dee Music (BMI)
see Jobete Music Co.

Foster Frees Music Inc. (BMI)
c/o Shankman De Blasio
740 N. La Brea Ave.
Los Angeles, California 90038

Fresh Avery Music (BMI)
see Sony ATV Music

Fugue Music (BMI)
PO Box 163870
Austin, Texas 78716

Full Keel Music (ASCAP)
9320 Wilshire Blvd., Ste. 200
Beverly Hills, California 90212

Funky Stix Music (BMI)
see EMI Music Publishing

Furious Rose (BMI)
500 5th Ave., Ste. 2800
New York, New York 10110

G

G. I. Music (BMI)
see John Doe Music

Gangsta Boogie (ASCAP)
see Warner-Chappell Music

Kelly Garrett Music (BMI)
see Almo/Irving Music

Gasoline Alley Music (BMI)
see MCA Music

David Gavurin (England) (BMI)
Address Unavailable

Gee Street Music (ASCAP)
see Ensign Music

Gemrod Music, Inc. (BMI)
c/o Walter Hofer
221 W. 57th St.
New York, New York 10019

Get Into Magic (ASCAP)
see Warner-Chappell Music

Gibb Brothers Music (BMI)
see BMG Music

G.I.D. Music (ASCAP)
PO Box 120249
Nashville, Tennessee 37212

Godfather Music (BMI)
see BMG Music

Godhap Music (BMI)
see EMI Music Publishing

Goldline Music Inc. (ASCAP)
see Warner-Chappell Music

Gorno Music (ASCAP)
c/o Alan N. Skiena, Esq.
1775 Broadway
New York, New York 10007

Grand Negaz Music (BMI)
see BMG Music

Great Broad Music (BMI)
see Longitude Music

Green Daze (ASCAP)
see Warner-Chappell Music

Guycol Music (ASCAP)
see Nick-O-Val Music

H

Half Mine Music (BMI)
see EMI Music Publishing

Rick Hall Music (ASCAP)
PO Box 2527
603 E. Avalon Ave.
Muscle Shoals, Alabama 35662

Hampshire House Publishing Corp. (ASCAP)
see TRO-Cromwell Music Inc.

Hamstein Cumberland (BMI)
1033 18th Ave. S.
Nashville, Tennessee 37212

Happ Dog Music (BMI)
see BMG Music

Happy Valley Music (BMI)
see Devachan Music

Harms, Inc. (ASCAP)
488 Madison Ave.
New York, New York 10022

Head with Wings Music (BMI)
see Pubco Music

Heart of Hearts Music (BMI)
see Windswept Pacific

Heavy Harmony Music (ASCAP)
see MCA Music

Heavy Rotation Music (BMI)
see BMG Music

Hellmaymen (BMI)
see Warner-Chappell Music

Henchmen Music (BMI)
see EMI Music Publishing

HGL Music (ASCAP)
see MCA Music

Hidden Pun Music (BMI)
1841 Broadway
New York, New York 10023

High Priest Music (BMI)
see Ensign Music

Hillbillion Music (BMI)
see MCA Music

Hingface Music (BMI)
see Ensign Music

Hipp Row Music (ASCAP)
see EMI Music Publishing

Honey Jars & Diapers Music (ASCAP)
see EMI Music Publishing

Hook 'N B (ASCAP)
see CBS Songs Ltd.

Hookman Music (ASCAP)
see Zomba Music

Hori Pro America (BMI)
see Polygram Music Publishing Inc.

Hornbill Music (BMI)
see Polygram Music Publishing Inc.

Hot Hooks Music (BMI)
see Of Music

House of Fun Music (BMI)
1348 Lexington Ave.
New York, New York 10128

Human Rhythm (BMI)
see Chrysalis Music Group

Humassive Music (ASCAP)
see Warner-Chappell Music

Hydroponic Music (BMI)
9595 Wilshire Blvd., Ste. 505
Beverly Hills, California 90212

I

I'll Show You Music (BMI)
see Bug Music

I'll Will (ASCAP)
see Zomba Music

Illegal Songs, Inc. (BMI)
c/o Beverly Martin
633 N. La Dica Ave.
Hollywood, California 90036

Incomplete Music (BMI)
1841 Broadway
New York, New York 10023

Interscope Pearl (BMI)
see Warner-Chappell Music

Intersong, USA Inc. (ASCAP)
see Warner-Chappell Music

Irving Music Inc. (BMI)
360 N. LaCienega Blvd.
Los Angeles, California 90048

Island Bound Music (ASCAP)
see Famous Music Corp.

Island Music (BMI)
6525 Sunset Blvd.
Los Angeles, California 90028

J

Jae'wans Music (BMI)
see EMI Music Publishing

Jam N' Bread Music (ASCAP)
see MCA Music

Lori Jayne Music (BMI)
1000 18th Ave.
Nashville, Tennessee 37212

Jazz Merchant Music (ASCAP)
see Zomba Music

Jelly's Jams L.L.C. Music (BMI)
see EMI Music Publishing

Will Jennings Music (BMI)
see Ensign Music

Jim-Edd Music (BMI)
PO Box 78681
Los Angeles, California 90016

JMM Music (BMI)
see Of Music

Jobete Music Co. (ASCAP)
attn: Denise Maurin
6255 Sunset Blvd.
Los Angeles, California 90028

John Doe Music (BMI)
139 Meadowlake Dr.
Hendersonville, Tennessee 37075

Jonathan Three Music Co. (BMI)
c/o Lefrak Entertainment Co., Ltd.
40 W. 57th St., Ste. 1510
New York, New York 10019

Steven A. Jordan Music (ASCAP)
see EMI Music Publishing

Joshua's Dream Music (BMI)
see Warner-Chappell Music

July Six Music (ASCAP)
see EMI Music Publishing

Jumping Bean Music (ASCAP)
see EMI Music Publishing

Junkie Funk Music (BMI)
see Warner-Chappell Music

Just Cuts Music (ASCAP)
see Warner-Chappell Music

K
K-Man (BMI)
see Sony ATV Music

K-Town Music (ASCAP)
see EMI Music Publishing

Kababa Music (ASCAP)
c/o Pen Music Group
6255 Sunset Blvd., Ste. 1024
Los Angeles, California 90028-7407

Keeno Music (BMI)
see Ruthless Attack Muzick

Keenu Music (ASCAP)
see EMI Music Publishing

Keep On (SOCAN)
see Warner-Chappell Music

Kejanda Music (ASCAP)
see Sony ATV Music

R. Kelly Music (BMI)
see Zomba Music

Kentucky Girl Music (BMI)
see Reynsong Music

Kharatroy Music (ASCAP)
see Chrysalis Music Group

Kids Music (ASCAP)
see EMI Music Publishing

Kiely Music (ASCAP)
see Zomba Music

Buddy Killen Music (ASCAP)
1307 Division St.
Nashville, Tennessee 37203

May King Poetry Music (BMI)
see Yam Gruel Music

Stephen A. Kipner Music (ASCAP)
Attn: Stephen A. Kipner
19646 Valley View Dr.
Topanga, California 90290

Kissing Booth Music (BMI)
see Warner-Chappell Music

Knob Twister Music (ASCAP)
see Reynsong Music

Kool Music (ASCAP)
  see Warner-Chappell Music

Charles Koppelman Music
  see Entertainment Co. Music Group

L

A La Mode Music (ASCAP)
  c/o Braun, Margolis, Ryan, Burrill
  & Besse
  attn: Malcolm Wiseman, ESQ
  1900 Ave. of the Stars
  Los Angeles, California 90067

Lac Grand Music (BMI)
  see Sony ATV Music

Lamartine (ASCAP)
  see Lost Lake Arts Music

Lambent Music (BMI)
  474 Old Bedford Rd.
  Concord, Massachusetts 02742

Largo Music, Inc. (ASCAP)
  425 Park Ave.
  New York, New York 10022

LBN Music (ASCAP)
  see EMI Music Publishing

Leaving Hope Music (ASCAP)
  see TVT

Legation Music (BMI)
  425 Park Ave.
  New York, New York 10022

Leiper's Fork Music (BMI)
  see Snow Lion Music

Lek Ratt Music (ASCAP)
  see Boo Daddy Music

Lennoxa Music (ASCAP)
  see BMG Music

Leo Song (England) (ASCAP)
  Address Unavailable

Lev-a-Tunes (ASCAP)
  see Bug Music

Life's a Pitch Music (ASCAP)
  see EMI Music Publishing

Lil Lu Lu Music (BMI)
  see EMI Music Publishing

Lilly Mack (BMI)
  see Bridgeport Music Inc.

Linzer Music (BMI)
  see EMI Music Publishing

Little Rain Music (BMI)
  see Bug Music

Loco De Amor (BMI)
  1775 Broadway
  New York, New York 10019

Log Rhythm Music (BMI)
  see Millhouse Music

Loggy Bayou Music (ASCAP)
  1303 Saturn Dr.
  Nashville, Tennessee 37217

Longitude Music (BMI)
  c/o Windswept Pacific Entertainment
  9320 Wilshire Blvd., Ste. 200
  Beverly Hills, California 91212

Loon Echo Music (BMI)
  see Zomba Music

Lost Lake Arts Music (ASCAP)
  c/o Windham Hill Records
  75 Willow Rd.
  Menlo Park, California 94025

Lou Dog Music (BMI)
  see MCA, Inc.

Lowery Music Co., Inc. (BMI)
  3051 Clairmont Rd., N.E.
  Atlanta, Georgia 30329

Loyal Duchess Music (ASCAP)
  see Ensign Music

M

Maclen Music (BMI)
  see Sony ATV Music

Mad Dog Winston Music (BMI)
  see Warner-Chappell Music

Maelstrom Music (ASCAP)
  11 Sparks St.
  Cambridge, Massachusetts 02138

Magnetic Music Publishing Co. (ASCAP)
  5 Jones St., Apt. 4
  New York, New York 10014

Magoo Music (ASCAP)
  see Virginia Beach Music

Major Bob Music (ASCAP)
  1109 17th Ave. S
  Nashville, Tennessee 37212

Makin' Chevys Music (ASCAP)
  see Maypop Music

Mark D. Music (BMI)
  see Sony ATV Cross Keys Publishing Co.
    Inc.

E. B. Marks Music Corp. (BMI)
  see Alley Music

Adam Martin Music (BMI)
  see EMI Music Publishing

Marty Party Music (BMI)
  see Warner-Chappell Music

Mason Betha Music (ASCAP)
  see EMI Music Publishing

Mass Confusion Music (ASCAP)
  see Warner-Chappell Music

David Matthews Music (ASCAP)
  c/o Grubman, Indursky, Schindler &
  152 W. 57th St.
  New York, New York 10019

Maverick (ASCAP)
  see Warner-Chappell Music

Maypop Music (BMI)
  Box 121192e Cavender
  702 18th Ave.
  Nashville, Tennessee 37212

MCA, Inc. (ASCAP)
  1755 Broadway, 8th Fl.
  New York, New York 10019

MCA Music (ASCAP)
  1755 Broadway
  New York, New York 10019

MCA/Northern Music
  2440 Sepulveda Blvd., Ste. 100
  Los Angeles, California 90064

McNooter Music (ASCAP)
  see BMG Music

Megasongs
  see BMG Music

Melusic Music (ASCAP)
  see EMI Music Publishing

Merovingian Music (BMI)
  c/o Chris Butler
  266 W. 11th St.
  New York, New York 10014

Midder Music (ASCAP)
  275 W. 96th St., Apt. 32G
  New York, New York 10025

Mike's Rap Music (BMI)
  25115 Stanford Ave., Ste. 107
  Valencia, California 91355

Milene Music (ASCAP)
  65 Music Square West
  Nashville, Tennessee 37203

Milkman Music (BMI)
  see Warner-Chappell Music

Millermo Music (BMI)
  see Polygram Music Publishing Inc.

Millhouse Music (BMI)
  see Polygram Music Publishing Inc.

Mint Factory Music (ASCAP)
see EMI Music Publishing

Miss Betsy Music (ASCAP)
see Zomba Music

Miss Blyss Music (ASCAP)
see Starstruck Writers Group

MJ12 Music (BMI)
see EMI Music Publishing

Mo Swang Music (ASCAP)
see Def American Songs

Mo Thug Music (BMI)
see Ruthless Attack Muzick

Mob Control (ASCAP)
85 N. 3rd St., 3rd Fl.
Brooklyn, New York 11211

Modar Music (BMI)
see Windswept Pacific

Mokajumbi (ASCAP)
see Personal Music

Mondial Lazer Edizioni (Italy)
see Polygram Music Publishing Inc.

Mono Rat Music (BMI)
see EMI Music Publishing

Montalupis Music (BMI)
see Rondor Music Inc.

Moon Catcher Music (BMI)
see Polygram Music Publishing Inc.

Moseka Music (ASCAP)
940 St. Nicholas Ave.
Apt. 5E
New York, New York 10032

Mota Music (ASCAP)
PO Box 121227
Nashville, Tennessee 37212

Mother Bertha Music, Inc. (BMI)
686 S. Arroyo Pkwy.,
Penthouse Ste. 175
Pasadena, California 91105

Mountain Thyme Music (SESAC)
see Major Bob Music

MPL Communications Inc. (ASCAP)
c/o Lee Eastman
39 W. 54th St.
New York, New York 10019

Mr. Bolton's Music (BMI)
c/o David Feinstein
120 E. 34th St., Ste. 7F
New York, New York 10011

Ms. Mary's Music (BMI)
see Warner-Chappell Music

Murrah (BMI)
1025 16th Ave. South, Ste. 102
PO Box 121623
Nashville, Tennessee 37212

Music Corp. of America (BMI)
see MCA Music

Mustaine Music (BMI)
see Screen Gems-EMI Music Inc.

Muy Bueno Music (BMI)
1000 18th St., S.
Nashville, Tennessee 37212

Mystery System Music (BMI)
see Almo/Irving Music

N

N-The Water Publishing (ASCAP)
12337 Jones Rd.
Ste. 100
Houston, Texas 77070

NASHMACK Music (ASCAP)
see EMI Music Publishing

National League Music (BMI)
6255 Sunset Blvd., Ste. 1126
Los Angeles, California 90028

Naughty (ASCAP)
see Jobete Music Co.

Needmore Music (BMI)
4015 5th Ave. S.
Minneapolis, Minnesota 55409

Nelana Music (BMI)
see MCA, Inc.

Neon Sky Music (ASCAP)
see EMI Music Publishing

Ness, Nitty & Capone (ASCAP)
see EMI-April Music

Neverwouldahot Music (ASCAP)
see Sony ATV Music

New Agency Music (ASCAP)
see Warner-Chappell Music

New Columbia Pictures Music (ASCAP)
see Sony ATV Music

New Don Music (ASCAP)
see New Haven Music

New Haven Music (BMI)
see PolyGram Records Inc.

New Hayes Music (ASCAP)
see Don Schlitz Music

New Hidden Valley Music Co. (ASCAP)
c/o Manatt, Phelps, Rothenberg & Ph
illips
11355 W. Olympic Blvd.
Los Angeles, California 90064

Randy Newman Music (ASCAP)
c/o Gelfand, Rennert & Feldman
1880 Century Park, E., Ste. 900
Los Angeles, California 90067

Nick-O-Val Music (ASCAP)
254 W. 72nd St., Ste. 1A
New York, New York 10023

Barbara Nicks Music (BMI)
see Warner-Chappell Music

The Nine Music (ASCAP)
see Warner-Chappell Music

Nineteenoro Music (BMI)
15 E. 26th St., Ste. 1803
New York, New York 10010

Nineteenth Hole Music (BMI)
see Maypop Music

9th Town Music (ASCAP)
see Naughty

No Chapeau (ASCAP)
see Warner-Chappell Music

No Ears Music (ASCAP)
4153 Woodman Ave.
Sherman Oaks, California 91423

No Fences Music (BMI)
see EMI Music Publishing

No Intro Music (ASCAP)
see EMI Music Publishing

Notable Music Co., Inc. (ASCAP)
Cy Coleman Enterprises
200 W. 54th St.
New York, New York 10019

Notewrite Music (BMI)
see Sony ATV Music

O

O/B/O/Itself (ASCAP)
see Almo/Irving

O-Tex Music (BMI)
see Zomba Music

O.C.D. Music (BMI)
2150 West Ave., Ste. 08
Palmdale, California 93551

Of Music (ASCAP)
see PolyGram Records Inc.

Old Crow (BMI)
10585 Santa Monica Blvd.
Los Angeles, California 90025

Olga Music (BMI)
c/o Delores Jabara
135 79th St.
Brooklyn, New York 11209

On Board Music (BMI)
see BMG Music

One For Three (BMI)
see Warner-Chappell Music

1972 Music (SESAC)
see EMI Music Publishing

Only Hit Music (BMI)
see MCA Music

Onward (England)
Address Unavailable

Barbara Orbison Music (BMI)
see Polygram Music Publishing Inc.

Roy Orbison Music (BMI)
see Polygram Music Publishing Inc.

James Osterberg Music
c/o Bug Music Group
6777 Hollywood Blvd., 9th Fl.
Hollywood, California 90028

P

Paige by Paige Music (BMI)
see Cherry Lane Music Co.

Paniro's Music (BMI)
see EMI Music Publishing

Peer International Corp. (BMI)
see Peer-Southern Organization

Peer Music (BMI)
see PSO Ltd.

Peer-Southern Organization (ASCAP)
810 7th Ave.
New York, New York 10019

Pepper Drive Music (BMI)
see EMI Music Publishing

Perfect Songs Music (BMI)
see EMI Music Publishing

Personal Music (ASCAP)
see BMG Music

Harve Pierre Music (BMI)
see MCA Music

Pioneer Publishing (BMI)
1112 N. Sherbourne Dr.
Los Angeles, California 90069

Plaything Music (BMI)
see Almo/Irving Music

Polio Boy Music (BMI)
see Warner-Chappell Music

Polygram International Music (ASCAP)
1416 N. LaBrea Ave.
Los Angeles, California 90028

Polygram Music Publishing Inc. (ASCAP)
Attn: Brian Kelleher
c/o Polygram Records Inc.
810 7th Ave.
New York, New York 10019

PolyGram Records Inc. (ASCAP)
810 7th Ave.
New York, New York 10019

Pookie Straughter Music (ASCAP)
see Boo Daddy Music

Pop a Wheelie Music (ASCAP)
see Ensign Music

Hugh Prestwood (BMI)
see BMG Music

PRI Music (ASCAP)
see Polygram Music Publishing Inc.

Price is Right Music (ASCAP)
see MCA Music

Private Area (ASCAP)
see Warner-Chappell Music

Promiscuous Music (ASCAP)
see Warner-Chappell Music

PSO Ltd. (ASCAP)
see Peer-Southern Organization

PSO Music (ASCAP)
see Peer-Southern Organization

Pubco Music (BMI)
Times Bldg., Ste. 200
Ardmore, Pennsylvania 19003

Q

Quadrasound Music (BMI)
see Warner-Chappell Music

Queen Pen Music (ASCAP)
see Zomba Music

R

Ramp Music (BMI)
see Warner-Chappell Music

Rancho Belita Music (BMI)
see Warner-Chappell Music

Ranger Bob Music (ASCAP)
see Polygram Music Publishing Inc.

Raw Cast Music (ASCAP)
see EMI Music Publishing

Real an Ruff Music (ASCAP)
see Warner-Chappell Music

Realsongs (ASCAP)
Attn: Diane Warren
6363 Sunset Blvd., Ste. 810
Hollywood, California 90028

Regatta Music, Ltd.
c/o Phillips Gold & Co.
1140 Avenue of the Americas
New York, New York 10036

Reifman Music (ASCAP)
see EMI Music Publishing

Rella Music Corp. (BMI)
see Warner-Chappell Music

Reynsong Music (BMI)
215 E. Wentworth Ave.
West St. Paul, Minnesota 55118

Rhythm Blunt Music (ASCAP)
see MCA Music

Righteous Babe Music (BMI)
P. O. Box 95, Ellicott Station
Buffalo, New York 14205

Rio Bravo Music (BMI)
see Major Bob Music

Robbins Music Corp. (ASCAP)
see United Artists Music Co., Inc.

Toni Robi Music (ASCAP)
see 2000 Watts Music

Rodney Jerkins Music (BMI)
see EMI Music Publishing

Golly Rogers Music (BMI)
see EMI Music Publishing

Rok Legend Musik (BMI)
2550 Laurel Pass Ave.
Los Angeles, California 90046

Ron Boy Rhymes Music (BMI)
see Warner-Chappell Music

Rondo Music (BMI)
see Almo Music Corp.

Rondor Music Inc. (ASCAP)
see Almo Music Corp.

Roshashauna (BMI)
533 Madison St., Ste. 3
Hoboken, New Jersey 07030

Rough Cut Music (BMI)
see EMI Music Publishing

Ruthless Attack Muzick (ASCAP)
3126 Locust Ridge Circle
Valencia, California 91354

Ryche Trax Music (BMI)
2020 Union St.
San Francisco, California 94123

Rye Songs (BMI)
see Sony ATV Music

Rysher Music (ASCAP)
see Warner-Chappell Music

Rysher Songs (BMI)
see Warner-Chappell Music

S

Sadiyah Music (BMI)
see EMI Music Publishing

St. Myrna Music (ASCAP)
see Major Bob Music

Salandra Music (ASCAP)
see Almo/Irving

Sam's Jammin Music (BMI)
see Sony ATV Music

Sang Melee Music (BMI)
see Warner-Chappell Music

Saunders Publications, Inc. (ASCAP)
119 W. 57th St.
New York, New York 10019

Sawng Country Music (ASCAP)
see Warner-Chappell Music

Don Schlitz Music (ASCAP)
PO Box 120594
Nashville, Tennessee 37212

Schmoogietunes (BMI)
see MCA Music

Scred Songs
see AGF Music Ltd.

Screen Gems-EMI Music Inc. (BMI)
6255 Sunset Blvd., 12th Fl.
Hollywood, California 90028

Scrogrow Music (BMI)
see Warner-Chappell Music

Second Decade Music (BMI)
c/o TWM Management
641 Lexington Ave.
New York, New York 10022

September Six Music (ASCAP)
see EMI Music Publishing

Seven Angels Music (BMI)
see Polygram Music Publishing Inc.

712 Stone Avenue Music (BMI)
see EMI Music Publishing

Shapiro, Bernstein & Co., Inc. (ASCAP)
Attn: Leon Brettler
640 5th Ave.
New York, New York 10019

Shark Music (BMI)
see Warner-Chappell Music

Sheek Louchion Music (BMI)
see EMI Music Publishing

Richard Shindell Music (ASCAP)
c/o Young/Hunter Mgmt
65 East St., PO Box 303
Chesterfield, Massachusetts 08012

Shoot Straight Music (ASCAP)
see Ensign Music

Michael Shore Music (BMI)
see Warner-Chappell Music

Showbilly (BMI)
see Sony ATV Tree Publishing

Sid Flips Music (ASCAP)
see EMI Music Publishing

Sidi Music (BMI)
see Sony ATV Music

Sierra Home (ASCAP)
see AMR

C. Sills Music (ASCAP)
see EMI Music Publishing

List of Publishers

Paul Simon Music (BMI)
1619 Broadway
New York, New York 10019

Siquomb Publishing Corp. (BMI)
c/o Segel & Goldman Inc.
9348 Santa Monica Blvd.
Beverly Hills, California 90210

6th of July Music (BMI)
see EMI Music Publishing

Skinny Zach Music Inc. (ASCAP)
PO Box 57815
Tarzana, California 91357

Sky Songs (BMI)
see Polygram Music Publishing Inc.

Slack A. D. Music (ASCAP)
see EMI Music Publishing

Slam U Well Music (BMI)
see Warner-Chappell Music

SLL Music (ASCAP)
see Sony ATV Music

Smokin' Sounds (ASCAP)
see EMI Music Publishing

Snow Lion Music (BMI)
3550 Wilshire Blvd., Ste. 840
Los Angeles, California 90090

So Bizzy Music (BMI)
see MCA Music

So So Def American Music (BMI)
see So So Def Music

So So Def Music (ASCAP)
see EMI Music Publishing

Son of a Gila Monster Music (BMI)
see Polygram Music Publishing Inc.

Sondaddy Music (BMI)
PO Box 128007
Nashville, Tennessee 37212

Song Island Music (BMI)
see EMI Music Publishing

Song Matters Music (ASCAP)
see Ensign Music

Songs of Jasper (BMI)
see EMI Music Publishing

Songs of Peer (ASCAP)
see Paige by Paige Music

Songs of Polygram (BMI)
see Polygram International Music

Songwriters Ink (BMI)
see Texas Wedge

Sony ATV Cross Keys Publishing Co. Inc.
c/o Donna Hilley
PO Box 1273
Nashville, Tennessee 37202

Sony ATV Music (ASCAP)
550 Madison Ave.
New York, New York 10022

Sony ATV Songs (BMI)
see Sony ATV Music

Sony ATV Tree Publishing (BMI)
1111 16th Ave. S.
Nashville, Tennessee 37212

Sony ATV Tunes (ASCAP)
see Sony ATV Tree Publishing

Soul on Soul Music (ASCAP)
see EMI Music Publishing

South Nashville Music (ASCAP)
see Warner-Chappell Music

Southern Arts Music (BMI)
see Spyder Mae

Special Rider Music (ASCAP)
PO Box 860, Cooper Sta.
New York, New York 10276

Spent Bullets Music
see BMG Music

Mark Alan Springer Music (BMI)
see EMI Music Publishing

Bruce Springsteen Publishing (ASCAP)
c/o Jon Landau Management, Inc.
Attn: Barbara Carr
136 E. 57th St., No. 1202
New York, New York 10021

Spyder Mae (ASCAP)
see Chrysalis Music Group

SPZ (BMI)
see EMI Music Publishing

Stacegoo Music (BMI)
see Warner-Chappell Music

Stage-Screen Music, Inc. (BMI)
c/o Careers Music, Inc.
Attn: Mr. Billy Meshel
8370 Wilshire Blvd.
Beverly Hills, California 90211

Stapp/Tremonti Music (BMI)
c/o Wind Up Records
72 Madison Ave.
New York, New York 10016

Starstruck Angel Music (BMI)
see Starstruck Writers Group

Starstruck Writers Group (ASCAP)
PO Box 121996
Nashville, Tennessee 37212

Steady Mobbin' (BMI)
see EMI Music Publishing

Steel Chest Music Inc. (ASCAP)
see Skinny Zach Music Inc.

Jeff Stevens Music (BMI)
see Warner-Chappell Music

Still N-The Water Music (BMI)
see Warner-Chappell Music

Still Working for the Man Music (BMI)
see Sony ATV Music

Stone City Music (ASCAP)
c/o Gary Michael Walters
8205 Santa Monica Blvd., Stes. 1-12
Los Angeles, California 90046

Streetwise Music (ASCAP)
5644 Tyrone Ave.
Van Nuys, California 91401

Strong Arm Music (ASCAP)
c/o 4th Floor Music, Inc.
PO Box 135
Bearsville, New York 12409

Studio Nomado Music (BMI)
see Sony ATV Music

Suffer in Silence Music (BMI)
see Sony ATV Music

Sugarbuzz Music (BMI)
see Warner-Chappell Music

Suge Music (BMI)
see Sony ATV Music

Super Supa Songs (ASCAP)
see MCA Music

Superhype Publishing (ASCAP)
see Walden Music, Inc.

Sushi Too Music (BMI)
see Warner-Chappell Music

Swag Song Music (ASCAP)
5 Bigelow St.
Cambridge, Massachusetts 02129

Swanee Bravo Music (BMI)
c/o Marty Panzer
500 E. 77th St., Apt. 1627
New York, New York 10162

Keith Sykes Music (BMI)
c/o Keith Sykes
3974 Hawkins Mill Rd.
Memphis, Tennessee 38128

T

T-Boy Music Publishing Co., Inc. (ASCAP)
c/o Lipservices
1841 Broadway
New York, New York 10023

Tam-Cat Music (BMI)
see Warner-Chappell Music

Tamina Music (ASCAP)
see Sony ATV Music

TCF Music (ASCAP)
see Warner-Chappell Music

Ten-East Music (BMI)
c/o L. Lee Phillips
Mitchell, Silberberg & Knupp
1800 Century Park, E.
Los Angeles, California 90067

Ten Ten Tunes (ASCAP)
1010 16th Ave. South
Nashville, Tennessee 37212

Tentative Music (BMI)
3125 Chesnut St.
New Orleans, Louisiana 70115

Terilee Music (BMI)
see Sony ATV Tree Publishing

Texas Wedge (ASCAP)
11 Music Square East
Nashville, Tennessee 37212

Texas Wedge Music (ASCAP)
37 Music Sq. E
Nashville, Tennessee 37203

That's a Smash Music (BMI)
see Mike Curb Productions

Third Story Music Inc. (BMI)
c/o Martin Cohen Esq.ite 1500
740 N. La Brea, 2nd Fl.
Los Angeles, California 90038

Three Boys from Newark Music (ASCAP)
see PolyGram Records Inc.

360 Publishers Corp.
see Warner-Chappell Music

337 LLC Music (ASCAP)
see Zomba Music

3EB Music (BMI)
see EMI Music Publishing

Throwin' Tantrums Music (ASCAP)
see EMI Music Publishing

tHUNDERSPIEL (BMI)
see Bug Music

Eric Timmons Music (BMI)
see EMI Music Publishing

Tintoretto Music (BMI)
see EMI Music Publishing

Tiny Buckets O'Music (ASCAP)
see Zomba Music

TLC Music (ASCAP)
c/o Mini Movie Music
CBS Studio Center
4024 Radford Ave.
Studio City, California 91604

Tokeco Music (BMI)
see Polygram Music Publishing Inc.

Tommy Jymi, Inc. (BMI)
c/o Dennis Katz, Esq.
845 3rd Ave.
New York, New York 10022

Tony! Toni! Tone! (ASCAP)
see PRI Music

Too True Music (ASCAP)
see Almo/Irving Music

Tosha Music (ASCAP)
see EMI Music Publishing

Treat Baker Music (SOCAN)
c/o NGB Inc.
579 Richmond St. W., Ste. 401
Toronto, Ontario M5V1Y6
Canada

Treble Kicker Music (BMI)
see EMI Music Publishing

Tree Publishing Co., Inc. (BMI)
see Sony ATV Tree Publishing

Treyball Music (ASCAP)
see Sony ATV Music

Tribes of Kedar Music (ASCAP)
see BMG Music

Trio Music Co., Inc. (BMI)
c/o Leiber & Stoller
9000 Sunset Blvd., Ste. 1107
Los Angeles, California 90069

TRO-Cromwell Music Inc. (ASCAP)
11 W. 19th St.
New York, New York 10010

Trottsky Music (BMI)
see Warner-Chappell Music

Truly Soothing Elevator Music (BMI)
see Warner Chappell Music

Tsanoddnos Music (BMI)
see Ensign Music

Turgid Tunes (BMI)
see Bug Music

TVT (ASCAP)
23 E 4th St.
NYC, New York 10003

Twelve & Under Music (ASCAP)
see EMI Music Publishing

Twentieth Century-Fox Music Corp. (ASCAP)
Attn: Herbert N. Eiseman
PO Box 900
Beverly Hills, California 90213

2000 Watts Music (ASCAP)
c/o Darrell Allanby
375 Mt. Prospect Ave.
Newark, New Jersey 07104

Tyland Music (BMI)
see EMI Music Publishing

T'Ziah's Music (BMI)
see EMI Music Publishing

U

Uh-Oh Music (ASCAP)
see EMI Music Publishing

Unconcerned Music (BMI)
see EMI Music Publishing

Undeas Music (ASCAP)
see EMI Music Publishing

Underachiever Music (BMI)
23564 Calabasas Rd., Ste. 107
Calabasas, California 91302

Unforgettable Songs (BMI)
see Fox Film Music Corp.

Unichappell Music Inc. (BMI)
see Warner-Chappell Music

Unidisc Music (ASCAP)
see Warner-Chappell Music

United Artists Music Co., Inc.
6753 Hollywood Blvd.
Los Angeles, California 90028

United Lion Music Inc. (BMI)
c/o United Artists Corp.
729 7th Ave.
New York, New York 10019

UR IV Music (ASCAP)
see EMI Music Publishing

V

Vanderpool Music (BMI)
see Famous Music Corp.

Virgin Music (ASCAP)
see EMI Music Publishing

Virgin Songs (BMI)
see EMI Music Publishing

Virginia Beach Music (ASCAP)
see Warner-Chappell Music

W

Wacissa River Music (BMI)
1102 17th Ave. S., Ste. 400
Nashville, Tennessee 37212

Wadud Music (BMI)
see Warner-Chappell Music

Walden Music, Inc. (ASCAP)
see Warner-Chappell Music

Kevin Wales (ASCAP)
see EMI Music Publishing

Wally Songs (ASCAP)
Address Unavailable

Steve Wariner (BMI)
c/o Siren Songs
Gelfand, Rennert & Feldman
1880 Century Park, E., No. 900
Los Angeles, California 90067

Warner-Chappell Music (ASCAP)
10585 Santa Monica Blvd.
Los Angeles, California 90025

Warner-Tamerlane Music (BMI)
see Warner-Chappell Music

Warren G Music (ASCAP)
see EMI Music Publishing

Chris Waters Music
Address Unavailable

WB Music (ASCAP)
10585 Santa Monica Blvd.
Los Angeles, California 90025

Webo Girl (ASCAP)
see House of Fun Music

Wedgewood Avenue Music (BMI)
see Windswept Pacific

Weenie Stand Music (ASCAP)
see Warner-Chappell Music

Weowna Music (BMI)
see Bug Music

We've Got the Music (BMI)
805 18th Ave. S.
Nashville, Tennessee 37203

Harriet Wheeler (England)
see David Gavurin (England)

Who's Your Daddy Music (ASCAP)
see Warner-Chappell Music

Wiggly Tooth Music (ASCAP)
see Warner-Chappell Music

Wiija (England) (ASCAP)
see American Momentum

Wildcountry (ASCAP)
see MCA Music

Kim Williams (BMI)
see Sony ATV Music

Jerry Williams Music (BMI)
see Bug Music

Williamson Music (ASCAP)
see Warner-Chappell Music

Windswept Pacific (ASCAP)
4450 Lakeside Dr., Ste. 200
Burbank, California 91505

Wino Funk Music (BMI)
see Warner-Chappell Music

M. Witmark & Sons (ASCAP)
see WB Music

Wixen Music (BMI)
see Warner-Chappell Music

Womaculate Conception Music (ASCAP)
see Almo/Irving Music

Womaculate Music (BMI)
see Almo/Irving Music

Wonderland Music (BMI)
see Walt Disney Music

Words to Music (BMI)
see Sony ATV Music

John Wozniak Music (ASCAP)
131 Crocus Ave.
Floral Park, New York 11001

Wren Music Co., Inc. (BMI)
c/o MPL Communications, Inc.
39 W. 54th St.
New York, New York 10019

Wu-Tang Music (BMI)
see BMG Music

Y

Yah Yah Music (ASCAP)
see EMI Music Publishing

Yam Gruel Music (ASCAP)
see Arzo Music

Yee Haw Music (ASCAP)
c/o Debbie Doebler
48 Music Square E.
Nashville, Tennessee 37203

Yeston Music, Ltd.
c/o Maury Yeston
21 Pine Ridge Rd.
Woodbridge, Connecticut 06525

You Make Me Sick, I Make Music (ASCAP)
c/o Manatt Phelps Rothenberg &
Tunney
11355 W. Olympic Blvd.
Los Angeles, California 90064

Z

Zappo Music (ASCAP)
see Bob-a-Lew Music

Zavion (SOCAN)
1948 Sasamat Pl.
Vancouver, British Columbia V6R4A3
Canada

Zomba Music (ASCAP)
137-139 W. 25th St., 8th Fl.
New York, New York 10001

ISBN 0-7876-1392-4

90000

9 780787 613921